EVERYDAY
HR

EVERYDAY HR

A human resources handbook for academic library staff

GAIL MUNDE

An imprint of the American Library Association

Chicago 2013

Portions of the Chapter 1 section "Principles of Position Analysis" were previously published as part of the author's article "The Basics of Position Review, or How Your Job Affects Your Pay," in *Library Worklife* (2008) 5, no. 2. Portions of the Chapter 3 sub-section "Coworker Support and Cohesion" were previously published as part of the author's article "Caring for Your Tribe" in *Knowledge Quest* (2012) 40, no. 4: 22–26.

Printed in the United States of America

17 16 15 14 13   5 4 3 2 1

Extensive effort has gone into ensuring the reliability of the information in this book; however, the publisher makes no warranty, express or implied, with respect to the material contained herein.

ISBNs: 978-1-55570-798-9 (paper); 978-1-55570-817-7 (PDF); 978-1-55570-818-4 (ePub); 978-1-55570-819-1 (Kindle).

Library of Congress Cataloging-in-Publication Data

Munde, Gail.
    Everyday HR : a human resources handbook for academic library staff / Gail Munde.
       pages   cm
    Includes bibliographical references and index.
    ISBN 978-1-55570-798-9 (alk. paper)
    1. Academic libraries—United States—Personnel management. I. Title.
    Z675.U5M86 2012
    023—dc23   2012018146

Cover and text design in Gotham and Chaparral by Kimberly Thornton.
Cover photography © Andrea Michele Piacquadio/Shutterstock, Inc.

⊗ This paper meets the requirements of ANSI/NISO Z39.48-1992 (Permanence of Paper).

*To Bryna Coonin, my friend, colleague, and ace reference librarian
who wished that someone would write a book to answer
her "everyday" HR questions.*

contents

Positions and Position Management 1

Supervising Others   85

Recruitments and Search Committees   113

Tenure and Continuous Employment   139

chapter 7

Concluding Thoughts 167

list of Illustrations

preface

ev•ery•day\adj\ : encountered or used routinely or typically

Every academic library employee, from the dean or director down to a student assistant, is subject to a number of complicated, confusing, and intertwined employment policies and procedures. Many of these are required by law or governed by federal or state regulations; other policies or practices are unique to an institution. Because of the complex interplay of these forces, human resources (HR) management and personnel transactions can seem mysterious or confusing.

Everyday HR: A Human Resources Handbook for Academic Library Staff was written to help demystify HR by providing basic explanations and rationales for the most common and practical applications of HR management in colleges and universities and, consequently, in their academic libraries. The book uses plain language to answer some of the most ordinary employment questions that many library employees have. While it provides a basic overview of HR practice in academic libraries, readers should note that there is a great deal of variance and latitude among states, systems of higher education, and individual institutions and their libraries in developing specific and local policies.

Although library managers and administrators will find *Everyday HR: A Human Resources Handbook for Academic Library Staff* useful, it was not written especially for them, and thus it does not cover organizational development or strategic HR management practices. Instead, *Everyday HR* was written for any employee working in any academic library, including supervisors, managers, and administrators, who may be new to these roles. Academic library "staff" refers to all the people employed by a particular library.

Organization

Everyday HR is organized from the reference point of the individual, that is, aspects of employment, specific laws, and HR policies and practices as they affect the individual in his or her roles as an employee. Each employee acts in one or more roles—as an individual contributor, a coworker, a supervisor, a consultant on selecting new employees, and/or an evaluator of faculty or professional colleagues. The chapters that follow address these roles separately and can be read either independently at the point of need or in sequence as an overview of the topic.

Chapter 1 introduces and explains positions and position management. A "position" is the building block of the library organization, defines what work is to be done and who is to do it, and is the basic unit for many personnel transactions. The chapter begins with a discussion of the concept of "position" and explains the difference between a position and a person who holds the position. It defines and describes the most common position status categories found in academic libraries, notes their similarities and differences, and explains how position status affects every aspect of an individual's employment. Position description, analysis, and management are covered in detail.

Chapter 2 provides a broad and general overview of the most important laws designed to protect employees. It begins with a historical perspective on employment, including common law principles of employment, and then presents key laws such as equal opportunity and equal workplace treatment. The chapter continues with explanations of occupational health and safety laws and laws designed to protect job rights, access to health care, and the privacy of personal information. These laws are equally powerful but are generally administered at the campus level and are especially important for library supervisors and administrators to understand. This broad view of national employment policy offers a framework for recognizing and appreciating the complexity of the HR environment in academe.

Regardless of an individual's position within the library or institution, all employees assume the inescapable role of coworker. Chapter 3 examines coworker relationships in the highly interdependent environment of academic libraries. Libraries are organized into functional work groups wherein every staff member relies on others to accomplish work goals and advance the library's best interest, and everyone is someone's coworker. The chapter presents theories of coworker influence, both for group support and cohesion and for coworker antagonism, along with practical ways to manage conflict and a discussion of coworker harassment and bullying.

Chapter 4 is devoted to the supervisor's role but is also useful reading for supervisees. Between the two, everyone is included, because everyone has a supervisor or reports to someone at a higher level. The chapter discusses the functions of successful supervisors, including achieving and maintaining expert knowledge in some aspect of librarianship, interpersonal communication skills, and the ability to solve problems or initiate group problem solving. Two important functions, motivating and coaching employees, are covered in depth, along with typical performance evaluation and progressive discipline processes. The chapter includes a discussion of toxic bosses, offering insight on possible causes of dysfunction, and a clear position on harassment and bullying. The chapter concludes with a brief discussion of personnel records and their retention and access at the supervisor and library levels.

Turning to the recruitment and search processes, Chapter 5 discusses the steps typically followed to fill vacant classified and professional positions and faculty/librarian positions and to hire student assistants. Each step in the processes is discussed separately, along with suggestions for planning the position, gaining authorization to recruit, announcing and advertising the position, screening applicants and selecting the best-qualified candidates, interviewing and assessing final candidates, checking references and credentials, prioritizing candidates, and making a recommendation for hire.

Chapter 6 examines the general process and specific procedures commonly adopted by many colleges and universities and their libraries in making retention decisions about individual librarians. Although the chapter is intended as background for those who serve on promotion and tenure committees, it is also useful for tenure-track librarians, library administrators, and anyone wishing to learn more about tenure and continuous appointment. Topics include the role of the promotion and tenure committee, guidelines and criteria for promotion and tenure illustrated with excerpts from academic library governance documents, conventions for the contents and construction of a tenure dossier, reviewing and evaluating dossiers, and general best practices for promotion and tenure evaluation.

Concluding with advice for all academic library employees, employees and managers alike, Chapter 7 suggests that most HR processes benefit from the consideration of multiple perspectives, a collaborative approach to problem solving, patience, and a willingness to ask questions. HR is a discipline best practiced in an environment of mutual respect and cooperation and from a shared perspective on the library's mission and objectives.

The book is informed by a variety of sources, including professional association documents from the American Association of University Professors, the Society for Human Resources Management, the Association of College and Research Libraries, the Association of Research Libraries, and federal documents from the Department of Labor, the Equal Employment Opportunity Commission, and U.S. Code. It also relies on sources from the literatures of librarianship, higher education, and business management. The book includes numerous illustrative examples from university and library faculty manuals or governance documents. Aspects of employment in unionized workplaces are discussed as they apply to topics within chapters, but because of the large number and wide variety of collective bargaining agreements, the discussion is limited to only the broadest applications.

Everyday HR: A Human Resources Handbook for Academic Library Staff is intended to demystify some of the typical HR practices that might be confusing or seem counterintuitive or counterproductive; suggest when and how they might be changed to benefit the library; and offer a perspective and platform from which individuals can search for their own answers. The author hopes that readers will find it to be an effective atlas of the most traveled regions of the HR terrain.

positions and position management

The position is the basic unit of all human resource (HR) transactions. Those who have worked in academic libraries for a long time may already understand how a position's status category defines and controls the terms, conditions, and protections of employment. Most employees know a lot about their own position category but less about others. It is useful to begin with a discussion of the concept of "position" and a broad overview of the most common position categories found in academic libraries and then discuss position description, analysis, and management.

The Difference between a Person and a Position

Every employee is an individual contributor to the college or university and its library, including the dean or director, and every employee performs the duties of a particular position. Some library employees supervise others or have librarywide responsibilities for a broad function. Because colleges and universities characteristically strive to be inclusive and equitable organizations, employees tend to view one another as equals or as equally important to the library's mission. This is a good quality, but it can cause confusion between an individual who is known and may be respected with the *position* held by that individual.

Think of a position as a box and a library organization as an arrangement of many boxes. The position box contains a written description of the purpose, responsibilities, and duties of the position and the knowledge, skills, abilities, and qualifications required to "hold" the box. Every time a document inside the position box is changed, the updated document is added to the top of the pile of previous documents. Over time, the history of the position is contained in the box. Every box has a number—the position number. An individual holds the box for a while but will return it to the library when he or she leaves the position. The library will hand the box to the next individual hired into the position.

Neither the box nor the person holding the box is static. Over time, the person might outgrow the box. The box might get too big for a single person to hold, or the contents of the box might need to be completely revised. The library might need more new boxes. When funding is short, the college or university might stop handing any of the boxes over to new employees (hard freeze), or think twice about handing boxes over to new employees (soft freeze), or take boxes away from the library permanently (reduction in force).

All the boxes are considered financial assets of the institution, because they represent money—the cost of pay and benefits for the person occupying the position. They not only represent the investment made to accomplish certain functions, for example, how many and what type of positions will be devoted to various library service and infrastructure requirements, but also structure and control work by assigning duties and responsibilities to individual positions. The administrative fuss over boxes and their contents and who's holding them might seem obsessive, but it is part of the mechanism by which responsible employers ensure that they can meet both their functional and payroll obligations and accomplish their missions in the most efficient manner. Colleges and universities that act responsibly will encumber, or set aside, a full fiscal year's payroll and benefit costs for each active position box. In effect, this practice "locks away" an employee's pay and benefits for the whole year and protects the resources from being spent for another purpose. If a position is unfilled for a portion of the year (the interim period of time when no one is holding the box) the unused portion of the encumbered funds (called salary savings) either belongs to the library or reverts to the college or university. If the funds automatically revert to the institution, the library might be able to request and might receive permission to use it for another purpose but can spend it only once (as "one time" or non-recurring money), because when the position is filled, the money will go back to pay salary and benefits.

The contents of the boxes are defined and controlled to some extent by the *status category of the box* rather than by the specific job performance of the individual who holds the box. Colleges and universities and their libraries need an endless variety of different types of positions and personnel to serve in many expert and supporting capacities. There are numerous commonly used status categories, and each has implications for how the person in the status category is hired, evaluated, and terminated as well as implications for the basis of compensation and work rules. Frequently used categories that describe position, or "box," status include exempt, nonexempt, tenure-track/tenured faculty, continuous academic professionals, fixed-term continuing, fixed-term temporary, and temporary/casual. Contractors, consultants, and independent service providers are *not* employees of the institution. They are service vendors. Although volunteers are not employees, they may receive some of the same legal protections that apply to employees, depending on state laws.

Types of Positions in Academic Libraries

It takes many diverse types of personnel to operate a college or university, so there are many types of employment categories. The broadest distinction has to do with the provisions of the Fair Labor Standards Act (FLSA), and every individual employee is either exempt or not exempt from the protections of the act.

EXEMPT EMPLOYEES

Exempt employees are not subject to the provisions of the FLSA; thus, they are referred to as "exempt." Exempt employees include faculty and professional staff members. The FLSA was created in 1938 to protect "blue collar" workers and has been modified many times since. The act was a product of the 1930s Depression Era and was touted as providing "a fair day's pay for a fair day's work." Initially, the bill established a minimum wage of 25 cents an hour and a maximum workweek of 44 hours, banned "oppressive" child labor, and set standards for overtime compensation. The original legislation affected only employers engaged in interstate commerce, but, over time, the provisions of the bill were expanded incrementally to cover most employers and to successively raise the minimum wage.

Exclusion from the protections of the FLSA is often referred to as the "white collar" exemption. Discriminating between exempt and nonexempt positions can be challenging, especially because library "collars" include many shades of white and blue—and a few other hues. There are basic tests to determine if an employee is exempt by virtue of executive, administrative, or professional responsibilities. The tests and related regulations take into account factors such as minimum weekly salary paid regardless of hours worked, nature of management responsibilities, advanced knowledge required by the work, judgment and discretion used, and whether the work relies on invention, imagination, or creativity. Some occupations cannot be exempted, for example, trade workers like carpenters and plumbers and fire, police, and public safety workers. To put it most crudely, exempt employees are paid for what they know, and nonexempt employees are paid for what they do.

Exempt employees are not restricted to a maximum number of hours worked during the week, are not compensated for time spent in business travel or professional development, and are not guaranteed fixed break and meal periods. They are not eligible for overtime compensation, because there is no overtime. Exempt employees are always salaried employees; that is, they are paid for the general value of their services

---

If someone is doing the work of a librarian, shouldn't he or she be paid for doing a librarian's job?

Regardless of FLSA status, if an employer treats you as an exempt employee, then you may have a claim to be compensated as an exempt employee. If a nonexempt person is performing the duties of an exempt position and has the qualifications required for the position, then this should be brought to the attention of the supervisor first, then to the library HR office (if applicable), and then to the library dean or director. The distinction between exempt and nonexempt positions can be murky, but there are "white collar" exemption tests and rules. The most recent version of them (2004) can be found at www.dol.gov/regs/fedreg/final/2004009016.pdf.

and receive the same paycheck no matter how many days or hours they work during a pay period. Exempt employees may not be suspended without pay for reasons other than the most serious conduct violations, for example, sexual harassment or workplace violence. Because exempt employees are not paid an hourly wage, there is no exact basis for using suspension without pay as a disciplinary measure. However, those in full-time exempt positions have a higher duty of loyalty than those in nonexempt positions. Because exempt employees are not restricted to a 40-hour work week, it does not mean that they are free to work fewer than 40 hours a week anytime they choose, or to set their own reporting schedules, or to take a second job surreptitiously. The general operating principle is that the primary commitment of an exempt employee is to the institution, and work responsibilities are not confined to any set number of hours a day, week, or year.

In libraries, exempt employees can include professional librarians, library administrators, computer professionals, development officers, HR officers, facility managers, and other specialized professions, in addition to tenured/tenure-track librarians and fixed-term or continuing academic professionals. About half of U.S. research libraries have adopted the tenure model for librarians, and about another quarter recognize some form of faculty status (Bolin, 2008).

TENURE-TRACK OR TENURED LIBRARY FACULTY

Tenure is an iconic concept, steeped in a culture all its own. The classic model of faculty tenure offers librarians a series of term contracts, either one year at a time or in multiple years that combine to equal seven years. If the probationary period is completed successfully and tenure is awarded, the tenured employee can expect to continue employment indefinitely and is eligible to apply for promotion. There are many variations on the model in terms of faculty status, rank, and method of performance review. In libraries, the main advantages to the tenure model have been to put librarians on equal footing with teaching faculty and to retain talented and productive librarians. These tenure systems generally award the same ranks as teaching faculty, that is, assistant professor, associate professor, and professor.

Tenure and tenure-track positions are subject to expectations for the quality and quantity of research or creative activity and for professional and community service activities in addition to expectations for job performance. This is the source of the familiar "publish or perish" adage. A tenure-track faculty member is considered a probationary employee for a very long time—traditionally five to seven years. Once probation is successfully completed, tenure is assumed to provide permanence of employment and afford protection from unfair dismissal, but tenure as a promise of lifetime employment has no basis in law. In law, there is no such thing as lifetime employment. Even Justices of the U.S. Supreme Court, who have an imperative need for protection against the sway of politics, can be impeached by Congress. However, many colleges and universities define what a faculty member with tenure can expect. For example, the Arizona Board of Regents (2011) considers that the award of tenure "creates a legitimate claim of entitlement to continued employment unless the tenured faculty member is dismissed or released in accordance with Arizona Board of Regents Policy. . . ." These types of published statements create the expectation of permanent employment and may have contractual implications, but they do not guarantee lifetime employment.

Similar to other employees on probation, the college or university can dismiss a tenure-track employee at the end of any contract period in the series of contracts. Generally, some notice that the contract will not be renewed is provided to the probationary employee in advance of termination, and the required period of notice may be specified in policy, but, like any policy, this can be changed by the policy-making body.

LIBRARIANS OR ACADEMIC PROFESSIONALS WITH CONTINUOUS APPOINTMENT

Although the language may vary, this status normally contains the words *continuous appointment* and is very similar to tenure. It means that after successful completion of a probationary period, typically five to seven years, the employee may expect renewal for successive appointment periods such as to constitute continuous employment. In some cases, continuous employment appears identical to tenure, but it might not include a requirement for scholarship or a lesser requirement for scholarship than imposed on teaching faculty, or it may use a different system of ranks, for example, Librarian I, II, III, IV or Assistant Librarian, Associate Librarian, and Librarian. Continuous appointment implies that the college or university has made a commitment to the employee but, like tenure, does not guarantee lifetime employment. For example, Michigan State University (2012) explains that continuous appointment status

> assures a librarian that she/he will not be dismissed due to capricious action by the Library administration nor will dismissal be used as a restraint on a librarian's exercise of academic freedom. Continuous appointment does not guarantee employment if positions are not funded, if there are gross violations of University or Library policies, if the librarian refuses to perform reasonable assigned duties or fails to fulfill contractual obligations, or if the librarian no longer renders satisfactory performance in his or her professional capacity at the University.

FIXED-TERM EXEMPT EMPLOYEES

These employees receive a term contract, usually for 12 months or an academic year, and the contract can be renewable or not. For example, when the position is paid from a term-limited grant, or when someone is hired to perform the position duties during an extended vacancy, there is a definite end date to employment. If the contract is nonrenewable, or limited to a specified period of time, then the employee is fixed-term *temporary*.

If, however, the funding source of the position is stable and expected to continue, along with the need for someone to perform the duties of the position, then the position is fixed-term *continuing*. In such instances, the contract is renewable indefinitely. However, fixed-term continuing employees cannot count on being employed beyond the contract period and are not eligible for tenure or continuous employment. It is important here to note the difference between *continuing* employment and *continuous* employment. Continuing employment is a commitment to a position, while continuous employment is a commitment to a person. Because they are not on tenure track, fixed-term continuing employees normally are not required to engage in research and creative activity, but they might be required to perform professional and community service. Infrequently in academic libraries, these positions can be called Professor of Practice and carry faculty ranks, but persons in these positions are not eligible for tenure or continuous appointment.

Graduate assistants working in the library can be best understood as fixed-term temporary employees. They are salaried employees paid for the general value of their services, but they are contracted on a semester or summer term basis. They may be rehired several times, but because they are expected to graduate and leave eventually, these are temporary positions. Fixed-term employees are sometimes referred to as "contract employees," but they should not be confused with contractors, who are discussed later.

NONEXEMPT EMPLOYEES

Nonexempt employee categories include positions classified within a hierarchy, sometimes referred to as paraprofessional, career-banded, merit, or support staff positions. Employees in these positions are subject to, not exempt from, the provisions of the FLSA, which define a normal workweek as 40 hours (or 80 hours within a two-week period). Hours worked over this limit must be paid as overtime at no less than 1.5 times the hourly wage or compensated by the equivalent value in paid leave. The FLSA requires nonexempt employees to be compensated at minimum wage or higher. Some states have set their own minimum wage that is higher than the federal minimum wage, and in these cases nonexempt employees must be paid at the higher of the two rates. For a list of the minimum wage set by each state, see www.dol.gov/whd/minwage/america.htm. The FLSA also specifies the range for paid break times during the workday (between 5 and 20 minutes) and establishes payment for on-call and call-back hours. Nonexempt employees must be compensated for travel time to meetings or training events not held in the regular workplace. Nonexempt employees are always paid on an hourly basis, and their time is accounted for on an hourly basis. Any of the 40 hours not worked must be accounted for by paid leave of some type, or the hourly wage equivalent of missed work time is deducted from pay. Because full-time nonexempt employees fulfill their duty to the employer during a set work week, they are generally free to do as they wish outside their scheduled hours—that is, to take a second job or work for another employer. This group of employees may be subject to suspension without pay as part of a disciplinary process. In position announcements and related budget documents, compensation for nonexempt positions may be stated in a manner that appears to be a salary, but it is not. The figure is simply the hourly wage multiplied by the number of paid work hours in a 12-month period (2,080).

In states with civil service systems, nonexempt employees may be considered state employees rather than employees of a state-supported institution or state system of higher education. That is, they are governed by state rules in addition to system, institutional, or library rules. State rules always take precedence over local rules. Nonexempt employees may be dismissed during the probationary period for any reason, but when the probationary period has been successfully completed, the employee is awarded some measure of job rights and may not be dismissed without due process.

Although good HR practice suggests that no employee be referred to as "permanent," the term is frequently used to describe continuous employment of nonexempt employees who have successfully completed the probationary period. The job rights include protection from unfair dismissal, a right to be considered for the same or equivalent positions within the institution, and perhaps the right to be considered for transfer within a state system. Permanent employees can be dismissed only for cause and only when due process has been followed.

Can nursing mothers use their paid breaks to express milk during the workday?

A provision of the Patient Protection and Affordable Care Act of 2010 amended the FLSA with regard to break period rules to require reasonable break periods for new mothers to express breast milk. These breaks must be permitted as needed by the employee, and if they exceed the paid break period, they may be unpaid. Employers are required to provide a clean, private setting for nursing mothers to express milk, and bathrooms are explicitly excluded as appropriate spaces.

Many states have passed legislation to detail or clarify exactly how the federal FLSA standards are met, to set additional standards, or to set higher standards within their respective states. Every state has a labor office responsible for enforcement of state labor laws. For a list of these offices and their contact information, see www.dol.gov/whd/contacts/state_of.htm.

TEMPORARY AND CASUAL EMPLOYEES

These workers are hired to fill an immediate but temporary need, and their employment can be terminated at any time. The most common example of temporary employees in academic libraries is student workers who are paid hourly wages. They typically receive no employee benefits, with the exception of Workers' Compensation Insurance, which is partially paid by the employer. The number of hours and the length of time a temporary worker can be employed are restricted to prevent employers from using temporary worker status to avoid the requirements of the FLSA or to avoid paying benefits extended to full-time employees. Student employees work fewer than 40 hours a week when class is in session because their primary responsibility is to attend class and study, not because the library or institution wishes to avoid full-time status.

Casual employees are temporary employees who are restricted in the total number of hours they can work during a 12-month period. Casual employees generally are individuals unaffiliated with the college or university who are hired to assist with seasonal fluctuations in work or to help during intense work periods, for example, during library moves or bar-coding projects. Casual and temporary employees usually do not hold a position box because there is no intention of permanence for the position, and the wages paid are considered a general expense.

Can someone have dual status categories?

Depending on the situation, it may be possible, but it's rarely advisable. For example, a student employee could not be a library assistant for 20 hours a week and also be a half-time nonexempt employee. That would be the equivalent of working a full-time position and in conflict with the purpose of student employment. When interviewing student applicants, it is a good practice to ask if they are employed elsewhere on campus. On the other hand, a person might be permitted to occupy a half-time nonexempt position and a half-time temporary exempt position at the same time, but this would be difficult to administer, for example, because of dual retirement systems, work schedule conflicts, conflicting overtime compensation requirements, and so forth. If there were a compelling reason to do this for a short period of time, for example, to teach a class or finish a grant commitment, it might be possible.

CONTRACTORS, CONSULTANTS, INDEPENDENT SERVICE PROVIDERS, AND WORKERS PROVIDED BY A TEMPORARY EMPLOYMENT AGENCY

These service providers perform contract work specified by the library or by the institution, but they are not employees of the institution. They are either self-employed or work for a private firm, such as a consulting company or temporary employment agency. Persons performing contracted services are not "hired" technically by the campus HR division or the library. Depending on the local conditions, they may be under the control of the campus procurement or purchasing authority and are typically considered independent employers in their own right.

Table 1.1

TYPICAL POSITION STATUS CATEGORIES IN ACADEMIC LIBRARIES

POSITION STATUS (WITH EXAMPLE)	SALARIED OR HOURLY	EXEMPT FROM FLSA	LENGTH OF PRO-BATION	TERMINATION
Tenure-track librarians (faculty status and professorial rank)	Salaried	Yes	Up to seven years	Anytime during probation, then only for just cause or financial exigency and only after due process.
Librarians with continuous appointment (faculty status and rank)	Salaried	Yes	Up to seven years	Anytime during probation, then only for cause or financial exigency and only after due process.
Fixed-term continuing (professional staff and Professor of the Practice)	Salaried	Yes	None	At the end of the contract period, but the contract is usually renewable for one or more years.
Fixed-term temporary (interim faculty or professional staff)	Salaried	Yes	None	At the end of the contract period, usually nonrenewable.
Nonexempt (paraprofessional staff)	Hourly	No	Six months to one year	Anytime during probation, then only for cause and only after due process.
Graduate assistants	Salaried	Yes	None	At the end of the contract period, usually one semester or term.
Temporary (student workers)	Hourly	Partial	None	Anytime.
Casual (packers, movers, security workers)	Hourly	Partial	None	Anytime, but mandatory when the number of permissible hours has been worked, for example, 1,000 during a 12-month period.
Library volunteers	Do not receive compensation in exchange for services	Yes	None	Because they are not hired, they are not terminated. The relationship can be ended at any time by either party.

LIBRARY VOLUNTEERS

The FLSA defines volunteers as those who render services without the expectation of compensation. They are not employees, and they are not covered by the FLSA. In some states, they are required to be covered by Workers' Compensation Insurance, or they may be required to sign a waiver or acknowledge in writing that they are not covered by Workers' Compensation Insurance. Library volunteers may receive nominal benefits, such as meals or small gifts in recognition for their services, and may be reimbursed for direct expenses, but they are not normally or regularly compensated.

Libraries cannot allow their nonexempt employees to volunteer, without additional compensation, to do the same or similar tasks for which they are employed. For example, library employees may volunteer their own unpaid time to serve as hosts or greeters during an open house or fundraising event, to bake cookies or staff a bake sale as part of a library staff organization fundraiser, or to sort books for a book sale. Nonexempt library employees cannot volunteer to work extra, unpaid hours in their regular jobs. No matter how willing they may be, nonexempt library employees should never be asked, or permitted, to work additional unpaid hours to catch up with a backlog of work, to fill in for absent employees, or to assume temporary additional duties. Every hour worked must be compensated. Table 1.1 provides a broad recap of the status categories of positions typically found in academic libraries with some defining characteristics of each.

Part-Time Positions

Academic libraries make use of both part-time exempt and nonexempt positions to supplement their full-time staff. Part-time positions can be temporary or permanent, but they are frequently temporary in nature. Part-time positions arise from a library's need to "bridge" work efforts during periods when a full-time position is vacant, for example, during a search or a freeze on full-time hiring; from "phased" retirements, when a full-time employee has agreed to a reduced appointment for a certain number of years prior to full retirement; to cover evening or weekend schedules routinely; or when the volume of work in a position is not great enough to justify a full-time position. In some cases, retired employees may return to work part-time when it suits both the employer's and the employee's needs.

The U.S. Department of Labor (2010a) reports that 25 percent of librarians in all types of libraries work part-time, and this figure is supported by King and Griffiths' (2010) identical finding that, by head count, 25 percent of MLS librarians working in academic libraries work part-time. Compensation for part-time employment generally matches hours worked or effort in proportion to salary; that is, 50 percent of hours worked or effort earns 50 percent of the full-time wage or salary equivalent. Benefits that can be calculated on an hourly basis, such as paid leave, can also be accrued in proportion to effort or hours. Other benefits with cash value, such as health insurance, eligibility to participate in retirement programs, and the employer's match to the employee's contributions, can vary with local conditions or policies. These benefits can be supported in proportion to effort or hours, or they can require a threshold for eligibility, for example, effort or hours at 50 percent or higher of the full-time equivalent. Other rewards and privileges of employment, such as eligibility for tenure or sabbatical, travel funds, training and professional development, and awards or recognitions may be restricted to full-time employees. These privileges are intended as long-term investments in employees, and the perception of return on these investments can be perceived as having less potential when extended to part-time employees. For example, it costs the same to send a part-time employee to a conference as a full-time employee, but the return on investment will be fractional (less than 100 percent) from part-time employees because they work less than 100 percent.

How Librarians with Tenure or Faculty Status Are Unique from Teaching Faculty

Librarians who have tenure or are on tenure track and academic professionals with continuous appointments are considered to have *faculty status*. That is, they are considered partners of the teaching faculty and share in advancing the educational mission of the institution. Faculty or academic status librarians typically are eligible to serve and hold office on an academic governance body such as a faculty senate or faculty council.

However, even librarians tenured as faculty and awarded ranks identical to teaching faculty are treated differently from teaching faculty in some aspects of their employment. Librarians may be referred to as "nonteaching faculty," and this small difference in terms can make it difficult, even for HR personnel, to interpret academic policies regarding faculty librarians. The nature of library professional work and library faculty positions requires some careful parsing on the part of those with systemwide, institutional, and academic division responsibilities for HR. The first significant difference is in the definitions of teaching faculty and faculty librarians, and the accounting and financial reporting rules that establish differences between them. All postsecondary institutions whose students receive federal financial aid are required to report financial and other data annually to the U.S. Department of Education through the Integrated Postsecondary Education Data System (IPEDS). In IPEDS, faculty members are defined as

> persons identified by the institution as such and typically those whose initial assignments are made for the purpose of conducting instruction, research or public service as a principal activity (or activities). They may hold academic rank titles of professor, associate professor, assistant professor, instructor, lecturer or the equivalent of any of those academic ranks. (U.S. Department of Education, 2012)

Teaching faculty are paid from the college's or university's instructional budget, and although the IPEDS definition reads as though it would include faculty librarians, it does not. For IPEDS purposes librarians are considered academic support personnel, and librarians are paid from a different budget category. Although librarians may certainly perform instruction during the course of their duties, the word "instruction" in higher education administration is generally code for "generates student credit hours," and instruction is only one aspect of teaching. Other teaching duties include student advising, serving on thesis and dissertation committees, revising existing courses and proposing new courses, and contributing to the overall design and management of program curricula.

Because of this (and despite the fact that librarians may perform for-credit instruction), teaching faculty are paid from the instruction budget, and librarians are paid from the academic support budget, which the U.S. Department of Education (2012) defines as

a functional expense category that includes *expenses* of activities and
services that support the institution's primary missions of instruction, research, and public service. It includes the retention, preser-
vation, and display of educational materials (for example, libraries,
museums, and galleries). . . .

These definitions and accounting categories follow the Governmental
Accounting Standards Board (GASB) requirements, and all governmental
colleges and universities use this budget model and its definitions. Independent postsecondary institutions follow a similar set of definitions
established by the Financial Accounting Standards Board (FASB). Further emphasizing differences between both library and computer professionals and postsecondary teachers is their series order in the *Standard
Occupational Classification System* maintained by the U.S. Department of
Labor, Bureau of Labor Statistics (2010b). Library and computer occupations are grouped separately from teaching occupations. Librarians,
curators, and archivists are one broad group (25-4000) and computer
occupations another (15-1100), while postsecondary teachers are a third
(25-1000) and are further subdivided by discipline. The classification of
librarians as academic support personnel also has implications for the
visa eligibility of foreign nationals, should the library desire, and be permitted, to hire foreign nationals, and this kink in the works is discussed
further in Chapter 5.

Where there is a union, the union may negotiate for faculty librarians
alongside teaching faculty, and a union contract might work around or
supersede some of the differences created by internal funding sources
or occupational codes. For example, if pay increases are legislated within
state systems of higher education, the legislation may refer specifically
to faculty appointed on an instructional budget line, and this would not
include faculty librarians or library academic professionals. A union contract may override some or all of the differences between federal definitions and accepted accounting principles and a union agreement.

Other embedded differences that make faculty librarians distinct for
some HR purposes arise from the librarian's 12-month appointment and
12-month payroll period (versus a teaching faculty member's 9-month
appointment but 12-month payroll period). Performance evaluation,
tenure, and promotion timetables or schedules can be slightly different
because of the 9-month and 12-month annual cycles. Personnel with

12-month appointments are usually entitled to paid leave days for illness, vacation, and holidays and perhaps to paid days for personal leave of some type. Teaching faculty receive no paid vacation or holiday time, and they generally do not accrue sick leave, although some leave provision is usually in place for serious illness. Long-term leave for teaching faculty is most often administered at the provost or chief academic officer level.

Being on a 12-month appointment can also make policies, such as reassigned time for research or service and sabbatical, difficult to interpret and apply to faculty-status librarians. Eligibility for awards or other recognitions may be reserved to teaching faculty. These fundamental differences between librarians with faculty status and teaching faculty can account for unintentional or perceived inequities or for misunderstandings among the library, the academic office, and the campus HR staff. The latter two groups might tend to forget librarians as a faculty group when making and implementing policy and in such cases need to be reminded not to overlook faculty-status librarians.

Position Description and Analysis

Every probationary and permanent library employee should have a written position description, and the position description should be reviewed and revised periodically. Maintaining accurate and up-to-date position descriptions is a management responsibility, not a responsibility of the employee. A position description is the key document in establishing a position's purpose, status, and level of pay. It describes the knowledge, skills, and abilities of persons who are eligible to "hold the position box."

POSITION DESCRIPTIONS FOR EXEMPT EMPLOYEES

Exempt employees are the "white collar" group that includes library faculty or faculty-status librarians or academic and related professionals. The fundamental consideration in position description within this group is specialization; that is, unless the library is extremely large, each position is somehow unique, and each position must be described separately. There may be several or many exempt positions grouped together within a public service department, for example, but each position will have a distinct set of duties, or a core set of duties plus a specialized set of duties, and an approved pay range attached to the position. Depending on the institution's flexibility and the absence of a union contract, the starting salary is generally somewhere within the pay range authorized for the position.

In some environments, the full position announcement used during recruitment also serves as the basis of the position description, and the position may be redescribed to one degree or another every time a vacancy is announced. In other cases, there may be a more detailed position description that follows a form used within a state, system, or individual institution. Regardless of the particular style used, the position description should contain the following standard set of elements.

Position Number

This is the number on the "box," and it is an inventory number used by the institution's HR and financial authorities to keep track of all positions—filled and unfilled. The position numbering system may be coded to budget lines or divisions within the institution and may serve a similar purpose to an item's acquisition number, that is, sequenced in the order of the position's creation across the entire institution. In this case, positions created earlier will have lower numbers than positions created more recently. Position numbering may not seem critical to librarians when seeking to make structural changes within the library, or to redefine a position, or to create a new position, but they are of great significance within the institutional and system environments. Numbering each position controls hiring, provides a relatively easy way to sort positions and payrolls across an entire institution, enables staffing studies over time, and allows the institution to track growth and development trends in the number of positions by their years of creation. Even if the library has money within its control to pay for a new position, a position number must be authorized and assigned by higher authorities. There may be a cap on the ultimate number of positions an institution or system is allowed to generate and/or a formula that controls the number of positions.

Formal Title and Working Title

A formal title is the job title the institution's HR and academic offices will use to refer generally to a position or a group of positions. For example, outside the library environment, but within the institution, positions usually have much broader titles, for example, Librarian I, Associate Professor, Associate Librarian, Library Development Officer, and so forth. Formal titles can be changed only through a process normally involving campus HR and financial authorities if the new title requires additional funding. In contrast, a working title is how the library decides to describe the scope of the position's responsibilities and how it will direct the person in the position to represent himself or herself to the library's public. Working titles indicate the specialization or area of unique responsibility, and the working title is what the person in the position should use in his or her signature block, on business cards, and when making business introductions. Working titles are much more descriptive of the area of responsibility within the library, for example, Information and Instruction Librarian for Sciences, Electronic Resources Librarian, Information Access and User Services Librarian, and Scholarly Communications Librarian. Working titles change far more often than formal titles, but the position description will always need to be updated to document the working title change and effective date, even if there are no changes to the essential duties or to the pay. When communicating with campus HR and academic authorities about a position, the position number and formal title should always be provided. Working titles can be very difficult for those outside the library to understand, and external staff may not even recognize the working title as a position assigned to the library or have a clue as to the function of the position.

Reporting Line

The reporting line describes a position's situation within the organizational structure (division or departmental work group) and the title of the position to which the subordinate position reports. Figure 1.1 illustrates a typical organizational chart for a library public services division. In this example, the Instruction Coordinator reports directly to the Director of Public Services but does not supervise any personnel. This type of position is called a "staff" position and is indicated by a horizontal line. The Head of Reference, the Head of Circulation/Access, and the Head of the Information Commons also report directly to the Director of Public Services. This type of position is called a "line" position because it falls along a vertical line in the chart.

Figure 1.1

EXAMPLE LIBRARY DIVISION ORGANIZATIONAL CHART

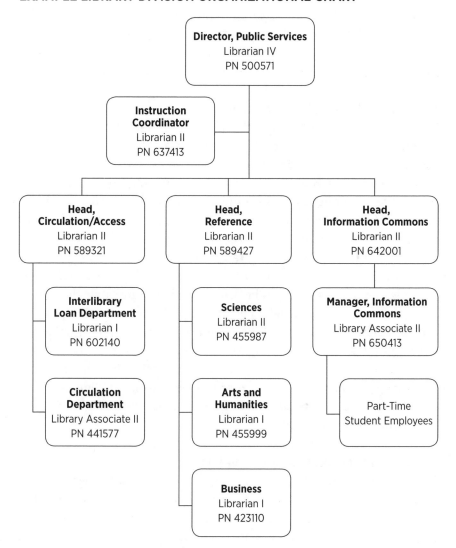

Scope and Nature of Responsibilities

This describes the purpose and the desired functional outcomes of a position, the level of authority and responsibility, and the library's expectations of those who might hold the position, and it can include specific
tasks or duties normally assigned to the position. A defining characteristic of exempt (versus nonexempt) professional positions is their basis

in functional outcome rather than routine performance of a stable and specific set of duties. The scope and nature of position responsibilities may be stated in only the broadest strokes. This allows for wide latitude in specific duties or tasks, which may be subject to frequent change, but fixes the broad functional outcomes for which the position was intended.

Knowledge, Skills, and Abilities (KSAs)

These are the required and preferred qualifications for the position. "Knowledge" is the understanding of a field or discipline gained over a relatively long period of study and may be demonstrated by formal degree preparation and previous experience. For example, the required knowledge level might be successful completion of an ALA-accredited program of library education plus one year of experience in a public service position in an academic or large public library. "Skills" are the measurable levels of achievement at a task or activity gained through practice or training. Skill can be measured by accuracy, speed, or success rate. For example, required skills might be using HTML or copy cataloging. "Abilities" are the natural or acquired powers to perform a mental or physical activity. Abilities can be "soft," such as analyzing and proposing solutions to complex problems or working well as a team member, or "hard," such as lifting 50 pounds. Required qualifications specify the minimal KSAs that a person must possess in order to meet threshold eligibility. Preferred qualifications are additional KSAs that are desirable beyond the minimum requirements.

Compensation or Range of Compensation

Include the minimum and maximum annual salary authorized for the position. This could be a range or level coded to a pay scale or actual dollar amounts. In cases in which starting salaries have been negotiated by a union, the hiring authority has no discretion in starting salary. In these cases, the starting salary is fixed and may not vary from the provisions of the bargaining agreement. In other cases and when there is no such restriction, starting salaries may be negotiated within a designated range.

POSITION DESCRIPTIONS FOR NONEXEMPT EMPLOYEES

These positions include library assistants, library technicians, computer support specialists, computer technicians, and clerical and administrative support positions. Because there can be many identical or similar positions within the library or across the institution, these positions are not considered unique. They share enough similarities to be described and classified into job groupings. The broad elements of nonexempt position descriptions are the same as exempt positions but are closely specified within a classification scheme. That is, the formal titles, the nature and levels of responsibility, examples of typical duties, and the KSAs have all been predetermined either by the institution or by a state personnel authority. The "duty set," which is a group of "duty statements" associated with the position, will tolerate limited variance and is often further described by the percentage of time and effort spent performing each duty.

These classification schemes are employment systems that order positions into a hierarchy with corresponding pay levels, sometimes called pay "grades" or career "bands." The object of classification schemes is to compensate individuals fairly across a state, a higher education system, or an institution based on the comparative value of the work performed. Classification schemes are administered by HR professionals who analyze sets of responsibilities and the KSAs that are required to perform the duties of various positions in order to classify them within an existing job series. A "job series" is a group of jobs related by occupational setting or function, for example, a museum series, computing series, library series, clerical and administrative series, and so forth. The library may have little or no authority in shaping the classification system or the job series within the system, but the library can shape the initial and continuing classification of positions within its own workforce by the assignment of duties to a particular position or to an entire group of positions.

What is career banding?

Career banding is a compensation scheme that categorizes jobs into broad occupational groups of "job families" and arranges them within minimum and maximum "bands" of pay. It is more flexible, responsive, and easier to administer than traditional "grade and step" schemes. Employees move upward within their pay bands based on new job duties and newly acquired competencies and skills. The midpoint of the pay band is usually set at the competitive market average pay for the occupation. Some state governments have adopted these more flexible systems to simplify job classification and better respond to employment market conditions.

As libraries adapt to an increasingly fluid environment, classified position responsibilities can change within a matter of weeks or months. The application of Web 2.0 design and development to library public services, mass digitization of collections, and expansion and maintenance of increasingly complex network systems have created the need for more frequent review of jobs. Cuts in funding and positions or positions simply left unfilled can force the distribution of tasks from professional employees to support staff. In such an environment of change, more frequent position reviews may be necessary to ensure that positions are accurately classified. Position analysts are the local level HR professionals who perform position reviews, and they have had to struggle to keep up with sweeping changes in library and information work, internal changes in library organizational structures, and wholesale restructuring of workload and workflows. When seeking to advance classified positions within such library environments, it can be very useful to examine job series other than the library series. Other series may offer more appropriate duty descriptions and examples of duties, higher compensation, and greater internal flexibility.

Principles of Position Analysis

Understanding the basic principles of position analysis can help the employee and the supervisor know when to request a position review, how best to prepare for one, and how to increase the chances for a positive outcome. Position analysts are experts in comparing and classifying levels of responsibility within and across the umbrella organization, but they are rarely experts in library and information work. A classified employee is usually eligible for a higher position in a classification scheme if two criteria are met. First, the employee must perform, or be asked to perform, the essential duties of a higher level position on a continuing basis and as a significant percentage of effort. Second, the employee must meet the knowledge, skills, and abilities requirements of the higher level position. The primary document for determining if the essential duties qualify at the higher level is the position description. Unless the position description is written or revised to reflect an upward change in job duties, no reclassification of the position is possible. The analyst will rely on the position description as the key document in making the determination. In some cases, depending on organizationwide procedures, the analyst will also study associated documents, such as a position "questionnaire," notes from separate interviews with the incumbent and the supervisor, notes from direct observation of work being performed, work performance standards that accompany the position, and individual position histories. Position histories are records of the position (not the employee) back to its inception date—the contents of the "box." The analyst will also compare the duties of the position under review with position descriptions on file for the same and similar classifications, for example, computing or information technology positions, executive assistants, and program coordinators. This helps ensure equity across the entire organization.

During the analysis, no information about the specific employee (work performance, attendance, or individual characteristics) is taken into account. The duties of the position are being studied, not the person who currently holds the position. Position analysis assesses whether intended or unintended changes in the duties of the position have tipped the balance into a higher position classification.

COMPENSABLE FACTORS

The analyst will usually consider the following five or more "compensable" factors to determine if the position meets the threshold for a higher level classification. Neither skill nor performance is considered in position analysis—only the duties of the position. The actual job performance of an individual should be compensated through other means, for example, merit or longevity pay increases. Compensable factors include only characteristics of the position.

Responsibilities of the Position

The most important considerations in the analysis are the nature and character of the position's major responsibilities. Essential functions, a term that also has Americans with Disabilities Act (ADA) implications, are those duties that a person was hired to perform, with or without accommodation on the part of the employer. An essential function or a major responsibility constitutes at least 20 percent of the time spent working in the position, is performed regularly, and normally is not delegated to another employee. A general rule of thumb is that at least 50 percent of the position's essential functions or major responsibilities must be at the higher level classification in order to reclassify the position. The analyst evaluates the difficulty and complexity of the work performed, the level of authority delegated to the position, the level of independent judgment exercised by the position, and any restraints on independent action. Difficulty and complexity levels are higher when duties involve nonstandardized, nonroutine work that requires problem solving, expert knowledge, and some degree of creativity. Authority and independent action are higher in positions required to make decisions about the work or work process and flow or to make these decisions for a functional group. In most cases, being the senior employee in a work group or a "lead worker" is not enough by itself to justify a reclassification upward.

Supervision

The number and type of positions supervised plays a role in position analysis. If the number and/or type of positions supervised have changed significantly, the position should be reviewed. Supervision is defined as primary involvement in hiring, evaluating, and disciplining other employees as well as directing their daily work, schedules, and activities. Employee supervision need not involve full-time, permanent employees. Normally, the positions supervised are evaluated as their total full-time equivalent, particularly if the part-time employees are responsible for a single function such as staffing a service point or performing a total major process or workflow from beginning to end. Such cases imply that the supervisor also exercises control over the function or process because he or she controls the workers performing the entirety of a function or process.

Position Impact

Position impact concerns the total effect of the position on the organization. Impact factors can include policy input or policy making, impact on the work of related units, and the level and breadth of the position's internal and external contacts. For instance, if the position is involved in legitimate policy making, or has major input into policy making, then its span of control extends beyond the work of the individual position. Be careful not to mistake control over procedures for control over policy. Procedures are routine steps in a workflow that can be changed at any

time to accommodate daily conditions. Policy is an established organizational standard that has been set to guide decision making. "Consequence
of error," or an outcome of error, may also be an impact factor. For example, a high consequence of employee error (costly in terms of the money,
time, and effort it takes to correct the error) indicates a higher responsibility level. If the work of the position requires regular contact with
high-level internal or external constituents, particularly those whom
the library wishes to impress or influence, then that position's impact is
increased. Anything that increases organizational risk has the potential
to increase the impact factor of a position.

Work Environment

Work environment is not usually a significant factor in most library positions, but it can have implications for information technology positions
and/or library security or facility maintenance positions. Work environments that are unpleasant, physically demanding, or potentially dangerous can increase the level of pay associated with a classification, as can
responsibility for the safety and security of others.

KSAs Required by the Position

Required qualifications for a position that involve special knowledge or
expertise or skills and abilities are often taken as broad indicators of the
levels of difficulty and complexity of the work performed. It follows that
the higher the position, the higher the required qualifications. Knowledge or expertise may be acquired through education or experience, or a
combination. A two- or four-year degree, completion of specialized training programs, or professional certification may be required for positions
at higher classifications. In some situations, educational requirements
may be partially or entirely "converted" from years of experience. For
example, two years of experience may substitute for one year of college,
or vice versa. Experience can be calculated as full-time equivalent years.
That is, documented volunteer work, student work, and part-time work
can be totaled and converted to full-time equivalency in order to meet an
experience requirement. Skills are measurable behaviors and generally
involve performance of a task with some degree of accuracy, speed, or
success. Abilities are natural or acquired talents and can be either "hard"
or "soft." To avoid disappointment, the supervisor should verify that an

incumbent meets the required qualifications for a higher-level position prior to requesting a review.

BENEFITS OF POSITION REVIEW

When the incumbent and the supervisor share a clear understanding of the position's current duties and the knowledge, skills, and abilities required by the work and together craft a clear, accurate position description, the review process has the best chance for success. Even if the attempt is unsuccessful, the supervisor and the library have demonstrated their commitment to fair and equitable classification, and the review process can be a positive experience. The busy supervisor may realize how the duties of a position have crept upward over time, and the employee gains a realistic idea of where he or she stands within the job series and relative to other positions in the institution, system, or state. When the review is a close call, the diligent analyst will have suggestions for adding or adjusting responsibilities to reach the reclassification threshold. If the position is reclassified upward, either or both of the following will occur: Compensation will increase immediately, or the compensation ceiling will increase immediately.

Position Management

Position management is the practice of managing filled and unfilled exempt positions to best meet the needs of the organization. It includes transactions such as merging partial responsibilities of two positions into a single position, recombining existing responsibilities to create new positions, redeploying vacant positions within the library, "swapping" the duties of two positions, moving an interested librarian directly into a vacant lateral position, or revising the responsibilities of a single position. It may include the management of a "salary pool," which is the money allocated for exempt positions to the library. A position can be repurposed or revised during a period of vacancy to reflect the library's changing competency, project, and service needs. Libraries may reorganize or restructure entire sections or departments, and this effort requires a considerable amount of position management work. Position management can be practiced only to the extent that it is permitted by the institution or by the terms of a union agreement. Some libraries have great latitude in terms of position management, and some do not.

Summary

Although people are the fundamental resource powering an organization, positions are the structural building blocks of an organization. To some degree, the number and types of building blocks control the composition and size of the library workforce, and their arrangement (organization chart) can describe the priorities of a particular library at a glance. Position description, analysis, and management are time consuming, yet continuous activities in most academic libraries. Modifying positions and their arrangement is a bureaucratic activity, that is to say, a rational and efficient method of directing an organization toward its mission and vision, as opposed to arbitrary or unfair methods that would harm people and eventually harm the organization. The next chapter discusses basic federal laws designed to protect employees and potential employees from harm—the people who are in positions or who apply for positions.

REFERENCES

Arizona Board of Regents. 2011. "Policy Manual, Section 6-201, Conditions of Faculty Service." Arizona Board of Regents. Last revised in April. https://azregents.asu.edu/rrc/Policy%20Manual/6-201-Conditions%20of%20Faculty%20Service.pdf.

Bolin, Mary K. 2008. "Librarian Status at U.S. Research Universities: Extending the Typology." *Journal of Academic Librarianship* 34, no. 5: 416–424.

King, D. W., and J. M. Griffiths. 2010. "The Future of Academic Librarians: A Ten-Year Forecast of Librarian Supply and Demand." Paper presented at the Library Assessment Conference, Baltimore, MD, October 25–27. http://libraryassessment.org/bm~doc/griffiths_josemarie.pdf.

Michigan State University. 2012. "Librarian Continuous Appointment System—Faculty Handbook." Michigan State University. Last revised April 13. www.hr.msu.edu/documents/facacadhandbooks/facultyhandbook/librarian.htm.

U.S. Department of Education, Integrated Postsecondary Education Data System. 2012. "Glossary." U.S. Department of Education. Accessed May 7. http://nces.ed.gov/ipeds/glossary.

U.S. Department of Labor, Bureau of Labor Statistics. 2010a. *Occupational Outlook Handbook 2010–2011*. St. Paul, MN: JIST Publishing.

———. 2010b. *Standard Occupational Classification System*. Washington, DC: U.S. Department of Labor. www.bls.gov/soc.

basic employment law

There are more than 180 federal laws intended to protect job applicants and employees from discrimination; to ensure healthy and safe workplaces; to protect employees when injury, illness, or military obligation interrupts their ability to work; and to control the employer's use of an individual's background, health, and financial information. Employers have some freedom to set the terms of the employment relationship but not to alter any terms that have been set by law. It is helpful to have a broad and general perspective on key employment laws. Becoming familiar with their intent and purpose can serve to inform library staff about their protections, help avoid error, and provide a background for understanding general campus human resource (HR) practices. This chapter begins with a historical perspective on employment, including common law principles, and then presents key laws protecting employees' rights. These laws are important for every employee to understand. The chapter continues with explanations of occupational health and safety laws and laws designed to protect job rights, access to health care, and personal information. These laws are significant but may be more important for library supervisors and administrators to understand because they involve management responsibilities. This broad overview of national employment policy offers a framework for recognizing and appreciating the complexity of the HR management environment in academe.

Foundation and Philosophy of Work in the United States

Because the United States has the one of the most contentious labor histories of any country in the world, there are very complex laws regarding employment and workers' rights. National attitudes about work have been influenced by more than 200 years of tension between the economic needs of the employer and the employee's needs for safe, fairly compensated, and satisfying work. Our natural history of work begins with the practice of colonial servitude and, later, the enslavement of human beings. It includes episodes of mass worker deaths in unsafe workplaces, children laboring in factories and mines, and the murder of union organizers and workers attempting to organize. Our more recent past includes episodes of discrimination in employment centering on race and color, national origin, religion, disability, sex, age, veteran status, genetic predisposition toward disease, sexual orientation, and gender identity. It is quite a striking history, and Americans have labored long and hard to transform the nation into one of the most enlightened countries in terms of fair treatment of workers. The struggle has created a society in which most knowledgeable, clever, and hard-working employees can achieve some measure of economic and personal success within the workplace.

More recently, our national workplace concerns have focused on the finer attitudinal points of such topics as equitable treatment of women and other protected groups, job satisfaction, wellness, health care access, work–life balance, and workplace "climate." Like librarians, most HR managers and others who work in the HR subdisciplines would say their primary job is "to help people." As a nation, we've come a long way, and our shadowed past accounts for at least part of the reason HR practice can be difficult to make sense of—most times when we've found a flaw or loophole in the employment relationship, we've passed a law to correct it.

In addition to complying with law and regulation, colleges and universities add their own unique layers of history, culture, policy, and practice to their HR management systems. Because of their education and research missions, colleges and universities attract experts in many disciplines and persons interested in the creation and transmission of knowledge. Therefore, their cultures tend to value expert knowledge, rational thought, and tolerance for intellectual and personal differences. They are typically organized as hierarchies, but they usually employ participative management as a broad operating style. Higher education offers some of the most inclusive, comfortable, and satisfying workplaces to be found. There is no lack of stress, ambiguity, and change in the environment of higher education, but in comparison to corporate and industrial work environments, colleges and universities are generally less intrusive. They have higher respect for employee privacy, disregard what might be considered normal expectations for individual employee differences and personal tastes, and usually attempt to interpret HR policies in the best interests of the employee. This chapter attempts to provide some of the broad principles embodied in U.S. federal law that describe the rights and responsibilities of employers and employees in most public and private institutions of higher education and, therefore, in academic libraries. States often amplify or add to federal requirements, and in some cases implementation is left up to the states, so this chapter should be considered informational only and not correct in every instance.

Common Law Principles in Employment

There are a few basic legal principles that apply to the employment relationship, and these are embodied in concepts of common law. Common law, transmitted from our British roots, reflects values and customs not necessarily encoded in law but that over time have acquired the force of law. The application of common law principles to employment is based largely on the consideration of employment as a contract between employer and employee. The contract can be oral, written, or implied by behavior. The most applicable principles in higher education settings are discussed here.

EMPLOYMENT AT WILL
Employment at will means that the employment relationship is voluntary and mutual. If no law or contract otherwise prevents it, employees

are free to quit at any time for any reason (or no particular reason at all), and employers are free to hire, dismiss, demote, and promote employees at any time for any reason. In theory, this might sound like a fair and balanced exchange, but in reality the employer has superior power in the employment relationship. If everything were amiable between employers and employees, there would be no need for the massive volume of federal and state laws enacted to protect employees.

There are recognized exceptions to the employment-at-will concept for both employers and employees, and they underpin many of the specific protections of federal and state laws. These include the public policy exception, which protects employees from dismissal for fulfilling legal obligations or exercising rights, such as serving on jury duty, filing for workers' compensation benefits or making claims of discrimination, refusing to commit perjury, and for "whistle-blowing." The public policy exception protects employees who are acting as law-abiding citizens, and it is for the public good. Two additional exceptions have to do with express oral or implied employment contracts. An express oral contract may be made when the employer appears to make a promise that influences an employee to do something or not do something. For example, a candidate is told during the interview or that she or he will never be laid off or will never be asked to work evenings or weekends as an enticement to accept a position. The statement may be truthful insofar as the interviewer knows, but the word "never" taints such a statement and could constitute an oral contract. If a statement is patently false and the interviewer knows it is false, then the statement could constitute fraudulent misrepresentation of the position. A promise or repeated suggestion that a promotion will follow if an employee takes on additional responsibilities or obtains additional training or education when it is known that no such action is likely could constitute fraudulent misrepresentation. An implied contract can be made when an agreement is implied by circumstances or behavior. For example, provisions specified in employee handbooks or manuals can be interpreted as implied contracts, and for this reason many employee manuals or handbooks contain disclaimers to indicate that the document is not intended as a contract.

Other exceptions to the employment-at-will principle are the duty of "good faith and fair dealing" and termination for "just cause." Good faith and fair dealing represents an expectation that both the employer and employee treat one another with honesty and fairness. For example, an employer who fires one employee in order to hire a relative would not be acting fairly, nor would the employer who creates and announces new work rules on a whim. On the other hand, an employee who lies about his or her qualifications or credentials or steals from the employer has not acted in good faith. Termination for just cause is permitted, but it requires following a process of discipline wherein the employee has a chance to improve job performance, and it requires following authorized termination procedures. On-the-spot termination is never advisable, and in most academic libraries a single person acting alone would not have the authority to terminate an employee, even under the most extreme circumstances.

NEGLIGENT HIRING, NEGLIGENT RETENTION, AND DEFAMATION

These common law principles affect the employer's duty to external parties or constituents. Negligent hiring or retention occurs when the employer knows, or should have known, that an employee was likely to injure or harm others—in the library or elsewhere—by being incompetent or unfit. For example, if an employee communicates the intent to harm self or others, then the employer assumes some liability for the employee's behavior if preventative action is not taken, and this is one of the rare times when termination outside the disciplinary process may be permissible. The most common actions taken by colleges and universities to avoid negligent hiring are to check candidates' academic credentials and business references, and this relates to another common law principle—defamation. Defamation can affect both the provision and the solicitation of employment references. Defamation is injuring someone's reputation by making a false statement out of malice, so giving a poor reference for a former employee is not defamatory as long as the statements are factual and not motivated by revenge or spite. Many states have "safe harbor" laws that protect employers who provide honest and accurate references for previous employees.

EMPLOYEES' DUTY OF LOYALTY

An employee has a duty to act solely for the benefit of the employer when engaging in any conduct that relates to employment. Although the scope of this duty varies by state, it usually includes maintaining the confidentiality of employer records, and this aspect of loyalty continues even after the employee has separated from the employer. Many institutions require their professional employees to disclose any conflict of interest between their professional and personal lives and to obtain prior permission before engaging in external activities for pay. The primary commitment of a faculty member or professional librarian is to the institution. This obligation applies to professional and managerial staff members and is discussed at greater length in Chapter 1.

Social media have created new opportunities for possible violations of the employee's duty of loyalty. Speaking ill of one's library or supervisor in a blog post, or leaking personnel documents or communications that were intended to be confidential, or advising an acquaintance not to apply for an open position "because this is a terrible place to work" may not be protected speech. In some states, there are statutes to protect library registration and circulation records, and sharing such information may not only violate those statutes but also violate the principle of an employee's duty of loyalty. The duty of loyalty, as well as other noted common law principles, serve as conceptual background and underpin many federal laws and court rulings that balance the rights of employees with the rights of employers.

Key Federal Laws Protecting Employees' Rights

These are the most basic guidelines for how employees are to be treated by employers and should be understood by everyone who works. There are numerous federal laws to balance power between employers and employees, along with regulatory agency rules for compliance, and numerous state laws that expand upon or further specify employment actions within their jurisdictions. There is an entire federal cabinet department, the Department of Labor, to provide oversight and regulation of employment. Because of this, it is impossible to cover all but the most fundamental provisions of federal employment laws and to cover only those encountered most frequently in higher education settings—laws that affect wages and hours, that protect diversity and civil rights, and that govern unions and protect their members.

Understanding the broad provisions of these employment laws can save endless time and effort, can protect the college or university and the library from the risk of error, can help library personnel know when to ask and how to frame their questions to their campus HR division, and can promote the library within the institution as a competent and positive employment unit. Maintaining superior collaborative working relationships with campus HR and academic personnel authorities benefits the library. In many cases, libraries employ the highest number of paraprofessionals in their institutions, and they employ the greatest variety of types of employees. In order to respond to rapid changes in the environment, libraries redesign positions, restructure or recombine functional departments, and reorganize more often than most other units within their institutions, and the ability to shape-shift relies on a strong partnership with campus HR.

WAGE AND HOUR LAWS

The Fair Labor Standards Act (FLSA) contains the most basic statements of wages that must be paid, sets meal and break times, and controls the hours that can be worked without additional pay. The act governs child labor and the federal minimum wage and sets the normal workweek at 40 hours. Because not every employee is subject to the FLSA, its most applicable provisions in higher education are discussed and explained in greater detail in Chapter 1.

Are student workers entitled to be paid minimum wage under the FLSA?

Not necessarily. According to the Department of Labor,

> the employer that hires students can obtain a certificate from the Department of Labor which allows the student to be paid not less than 85% of the minimum wage. The certificate also limits the hours that the student may work to eight hours in a day and no more than 20 hours a week when class is in session and 40 hours when class is not in session, and requires the employer to follow all child labor laws. Once students graduate or leave school for good, they must be paid at least the federal minimum wage. (www.dol.gov/elaws/esa/flsa/docs/ftsplink.asp)

Currently, the federal minimum wage is $7.25 an hour (or higher in states that have set their own minimum wage), so if the college or university has obtained the appropriate certificate, students should be paid no less than 85 percent of $7.25, or $6.16 an hour.

EQUAL OPPORTUNITY LAWS

The keystone civil rights legislation is Title VII of the Civil Rights Act of 1964, as amended, which includes the Pregnancy Discrimination Act of 1978. This is not the only federal law that governs equal opportunity in employment, but it is the cornerstone and makes it illegal to discriminate in *any* aspect of employment based on race, color, religion, sex, or national origin. Other important employment legislation includes the Equal Pay Act of 1963, as amended; the Age Discrimination in Employment Act of 1967, as amended; Titles I and V of the Americans with Disabilities Act of 1990, as amended; Sections 501 and 505 of the Rehabilitation Act of 1973; and Title II of the Genetic Information Nondiscrimination Act of 2008. These laws are administered by the Equal Employment Opportunity Commission (EEOC) and enforced by the Office of Federal Contract Compliance Programs (OFCCP). The laws apply to all educational institutions, including those whose employees are members of labor organizations, and to labor organizations as separate and distinct employers. Several other provisions of these laws and additional laws apply to institutions that receive federal contracts or subcontracts or that offer programs or activities receiving federal financial assistance. Financial assistance includes federal student loans and grants, so these additional laws apply to every accredited "college, university, or other postsecondary institution, or a public system of higher education" (U.S. Code of Federal Regulations, Title 29: Labor). Such institutions must be regionally accredited in order to participate in student financial aid programs. Additional laws protect the employment rights of Vietnam era veterans, disabled veterans, recently separated veterans, other protected veterans, and their family members.

Do equal opportunity laws protect student employees?

Yes. Full-time, part-time, seasonal, and temporary employees are protected. The EEOC is responsible for protecting student employees against employment discrimination because of race, color, religion, sex (including pregnancy), national origin, disability, age (age 40 or older), or genetic information. Student employees may have additional rights under other federal, state, or local laws, for example, minimum wage, overtime compensation, and discrimination on the basis of sexual orientation. For more information, see www.eeoc.gov/youth/rights.html.

The campus HR office is likely to have created policies and practices that control the steps of all HR transactions in order to ensure compliance with these laws and may have programs to educate employees in order to prevent errors in compliance or to avoid failure to comply. The reasons for these controlling policies may be transparent to library staff, may seem unnecessarily cumbersome, or may seem to slow personnel transactions to a crawl, but they are necessary for the legal operation of the institution. It is not unheard of for a college or university to be working under a conciliation agreement unknown to the general staff population, and this may account for additional checks and balances imposed on HR processes. A conciliation agreement details the good faith efforts being made by an institution to comply fully with equal opportunity laws. Such agreements can be the result of a previously documented violation.

In any number of specific personnel situations, more than one law may apply to different aspects of the situation. For example, in a situation involving a person who is 40 years of age or over and who has a recognized disability that may be related genetically to race or nationality, there could be four overlapping laws to protect the person from workplace discrimination. This is why HR professionals find it difficult to answer hypothetical questions; there are simply too many variables in play to give a sound answer. At times, these characteristics or aspects of an individual can affect an employee's specific work performance, but unsatisfactory work performance is not protected by any law. It is no wonder library supervisors and administrators have difficulty parsing out the intricacies of the many protections of employment law. The worst approach is to try to deal with difficult situations at the supervisor or library levels or to hope a bad situation will somehow resolve itself. The campus HR authority should be advised whenever situations become complicated beyond the level of expertise within the library so that HR staff can analyze the situation and provide specific guidance. Unless instructed otherwise, it should be assumed that *all* federal laws governing *all* aspects of employment apply to the library.

These aspects of employment include familiar HR transactions that require paperwork, such as recruiting and hiring, pay and fringe benefits, classification, leave policies, performance evaluation systems, promotion, discipline, dismissal, and transfer, but also include access to training or professional development and other terms, conditions, and privileges of employment. Conditions of employment can include such aspects as workplace climate (hostile workplace), treatment by coworkers, and access to the work premises, including parking and the location of work assignments, as well as internal procedures, such as adjusting work hours for religious services or observances or controlling negative speech or behavior directed toward a person's dress or appearance. Specific situations are discussed further as they apply in Chapters 4, 5, and 6.

Groups specifically protected from discrimination by these laws include almost everyone at one time or another, or sooner or later, assuming most employees will reach age 40. Although protected groups were established to identify those most egregiously discriminated against in the past, they now include persons of any race (including white Caucasians), religion (including Christian), sex (including male), or national origin (by birth or derivation). Also protected from discrimination are individuals with disabilities, individuals 40 or older (and who are protected until death), persons with genetic predisposition(s) toward diseases or disorders, and members or former members of the armed services. Additionally, employees who have complained about discrimination, filed a charge of discrimination, or participated in an employment discrimination investigation or lawsuit are protected from retaliation. By 2009, 13 states and the District of Columbia had laws prohibiting discrimination against persons due to sexual orientation or gender identity/expression, and eight additional states had laws prohibiting discrimination against persons due to sexual orientation but not gender identity (National Gay and Lesbian Task Force, 2009). In 2009, a bill was introduced in Congress, HR 2981, the Employment Non-Discrimination Act of 2009 (ENDA), that would prohibit employment discrimination against persons based on perceived or actual sexual orientation or gender identity (U.S. Congress, House, 2009). The bill eventually died and there is no national law protecting these groups.

Perhaps the simplest way to stay on the right side of present and future laws designed to prevent discrimination is to focus on their intent and adopt a personal operating code based not on learning who is protected, but also on protecting everyone—and everyone is anyone who is not you. This may sound blindly simplistic, but it is much easier to consider every person protected from discrimination against the inescapable and uncontrollable aspects of being human rather than to attempt to understand how every law applies or might be adjudicated in every situation. There are simply too many variables in most employment situations to effectively determine exactly what the law requires. People have native characteristics, either present at birth or acquired during life, and these characteristics may or may not be related to their ability to perform a job. If one or more of these characteristics proves to be an impossible barrier to job performance, then the characteristic is the barrier, not discrimination. However, it may not be assumed that the characteristic is necessarily a barrier to job performance, but neither is it required to permit a person to do less work, easier work, or less satisfactory work, or to disregard any other legitimate work rule because of the characteristic. One employment lawyer puts it this way:

> Can you reject an applicant for a driver position because she is blind? No. But you can reject her because she cannot drive. Focus on skills and abilities—not disabilities. . . . Always ask yourself if the factor truly relates to an individual's ability to perform the essential functions of the job. If the answer is "no," then don't take it into consideration, even if the law neglects to protect it. (Segal, 2010)

Discrimination may be more subtle than apparent, or it may not be noticeable over short periods of time. It involves both discrete actions and patterns of action. For example, two employees apply for the same promotion; one is white and one is African American, and they both appear to be equally qualified. If the white employee is given the promotion, is this discrimination? It might or might not be, but if, over time, African Americans aren't promoted at the same rate as whites, it's likely that discrimination has become an established practice, and that practice violates the law. What if only African Americans with lighter skin tones or other race-linked characteristics (hair texture or facial features) considered "attractive" were promoted more than other African Americans? This would also violate the law, which protects persons of all colors no matter their racial group membership. What if white persons who were married to African American persons were promoted less frequently than members of same-race couples? That would also violate the law. What if there is no conscious intention to practice discrimination or discrimination actually seems like a positive practice? For example, if the staff of a branch library or collection devoted to African American history (or another racial group's history) is composed solely of African Americans, this could be the outcome of assuming that African American librarians are uniquely qualified to hold these positions because of their race, which is a discriminatory practice. What if an entire department, over time, had become dominated by a single racial, religious, sex, or age group? It may seem like a natural tendency for staff to be more comfortable working with people who are similar to existing group members, but this could be a discriminatory practice. What if a person speaks with an accent that may be difficult to understand or that makes coworkers uncomfortable, so he or she is not given collaborative or visible roles within the library? This is a more subtle form of discrimination that may relate to national origin and could violate the law because the person is not receiving desirable work assignments based on national origin.

THE RIGHT TO ORGANIZE

Employees of private colleges and universities have the right to self-organize and form or join a union, and this right was established by the National Labor Relations Act of 1935. The act provided the basic guarantee of workers to organize, form, join, or assist labor organizations, bargain collectively, and engage in activities united in pursuit of a common goal (referred to as "concerted activity"). It limits the actions employers may take to inhibit employees from organizing, bargaining collectively, or striking. Along with other groups, the act excluded public employees at the federal, state, and local levels. In 1962, President Kennedy's Executive Order 10988 recognized the right of federal employees to organize, and some states followed suit using the National Labor Relations Act as a model, although the specific provisions vary by state. According to the U.S. Department of Labor (2012), the union membership rate for public sector workers (37 percent) is now substantially higher than the rate for private sector workers (6.9 percent), and workers in education, training, and library occupations have the highest unionization rate of all (36.8 percent).

American Rights at Work (2008: 11), a nonprofit organization, provides a broad overview of states with collective bargaining rights for public employees:

> Today, many of these employees have such rights granted in federal and state statutes. 26 states provide rights to public employees; 12 states reserve these rights to certain groups of public employees, like firefighters and those employed in education; and 13 states do not grant collective bargaining rights to any of their public employees.
>
> The Federal Service Labor Management Relations Statute provides these rights to many federal employees, particularly a large portion of the executive branch agencies. A slim majority of states

also have statutes providing these rights to one or more categories of public employees.

As of November 2006, the following 25 states—as well as the District of Columbia—provided collective bargaining rights to all public employees: Alaska, California, Connecticut, Delaware, Florida, Hawaii, Illinois, Iowa, Massachusetts, Maine, Michigan, Minnesota, Montana, Nebraska, New Hampshire, New Jersey, New York, Ohio, Oregon, Pennsylvania, Rhode Island, South Dakota, Vermont, Washington, and Wisconsin.

The following 12 states provided rights to some of their public employees, such as firefighters and teachers: Georgia, Idaho, Indiana, Kansas, Kentucky, Maryland, Missouri, Nevada, North Dakota, Oklahoma, Tennessee, and Wyoming.

By contrast, the following 13 states did not grant collective bargaining rights to their public employees: Alabama, Arizona, Arkansas, Colorado, Louisiana, Mississippi, New Mexico, North Carolina, South Carolina, Texas, Virginia, West Virginia, and Utah.

The 2006 *Directory of Faculty Contracts and Bargaining Agents in Institutions of Higher Education* reports that 94 percent of organized faculty are employed in public institutions and are concentrated in California, New York, and New Jersey (National Center for Collective Bargaining in Higher Education and the Professions, 2006). Eighty-nine percent of organized faculty are represented by one of the three most prominent unions in higher education: The American Association of University Professors (AAUP), the American Federation of Teachers (AFT), and the National Educational Association (NEA).

In colleges and universities whose teaching faculties participate in a union, librarians typically participate in the same organization and are covered by the same bargaining agreement. In 2008, the Association of College and Research Libraries (ACRL) reaffirmed its guideline on collective bargaining, the full text of which is, "The policy of the Association of College and Research Libraries is that academic librarians shall be included on the same basis as their faculty colleagues in units for collective bargaining. Such units shall be guided by the standards and guidelines of ACRL pertaining to faculty and academic status."

According to Applegate (2009: 451), about 19 percent of 1,904 academic libraries participating in the 2004 National Center for Education Statistics Academic Library Survey had unions representing librarians and faculty. McCook (2009: 5346) provides a useful list by state of academic libraries and the unions representing their librarians, along with links to their locals' websites. Nonacademic library staff may be represented by other unions, the largest of which is the American Federation of State, County, and Municipal Employees (AFSCME), and a single library may have staff represented by several different unions and who are working under several different contracts.

To cast the union environment very broadly in terms of HR operations, all compensation and benefits, hours of work and number of days to be worked, disciplinary procedures, grievance procedures, entitlements to jobs (seniority), and layoff rules are negotiated and specified in multiyear contracts. Union contracts generally do not recognize individual merit as a compensable factor; that is, the same pay is negotiated collectively for employees doing the same job. Individuals' salaries at hire are not negotiated with library management. Because compensation is fixed within the terms of a union contract, no variation would be permitted.

ENFORCEMENT AGENCIES

Because the laws are numerous and broad, and some expand on or overlap others, they require several agencies to ensure proper administration of all aspects of the laws. The agencies identified here have enforcement power across civil rights laws and orders and other laws that protect applicants, employees, and former employees from discrimination. The agencies issue guidelines for compliance and coordinate their activities with one another through mutual agreements, called MOUs.

The Equal Employment Opportunity Commission (EEOC) is a bipartisan policy-making commission composed of five presidentially appointed members. The commission is responsible for enforcing federal laws that make it illegal to discriminate against a job applicant or an employee because of the person's race, color, religion, sex, national origin, disability, or genetic information. The EEOC investigates charges of discrimination against employers through its 53 field offices throughout the United States.

The Office of Federal Contract Compliance Programs (OFCCP) is a section of the Department of Labor. Its mission is to enforce the contractual promise of affirmative action and equal employment opportunity required of organizations doing business with the federal government. The OFCCP offers technical assistance to employers, investigates complaints, and performs compliance evaluations or "audits." In cases where violations are found, the OFCCP obtains conciliation agreements and monitors employers' progress throughout the compliance process. The OFCCP has a well-earned reputation for strict enforcement of the law, and it has broad power to interpret law. One difference between the EEOC and the OFCCP is that the EEOC investigates complaints, while the OFCCP investigates complaints and also performs compliance audits independent of complaints.

The Veterans Employment and Training Service (VETS), a part of the Department of Labor, investigates and attempts to resolve complaints of Uniformed Services Employment and Reemployment Rights Act violations, and it is authorized to refer cases to the Department of Justice or the Department of Labor's Office of Special Counsel.

The Employment Litigation Section of the Department of Justice enforces against state and local government employers (which would include state-supported institutions) the provisions of Title VII of the Civil Rights Act of 1964, as amended, and other federal laws prohibiting employment practices that discriminate on grounds of race, sex, religion, and national origin. The Section also enforces against state and local government employers and private employers according to the Uniformed Services Employment and Reemployment Rights Act.

The National Labor Relations Board (NLRB) enforces the National Labor Relations Act. The Board is composed of five members appointed by the President and acts as a quasi-judicial body. The NLRB conducts elections to determine union representations, investigates charges of unfair labor practices by employers and unions, represents the party making a charge, seeks resolution, and enforces orders.

This section enumerated and explained some of the most basic legal protections as "ground rules" for establishing and maintaining employment relationships that are fair, are free from discrimination, and allow employees to determine and follow their own best interests in the workplace. Table 2.1 summarizes the major federal laws that protect these employee rights.

Table 2.1

KEY FEDERAL LAWS PROTECTING EMPLOYEES' RIGHTS

FEDERAL LAW	PURPOSE
Title VII of the Civil Rights Act of 1964, as amended	This makes it illegal to discriminate in *any* aspect of employment based on race, color, religion, sex, or national origin. Broad aspects of employment include hiring, promotion, discharge, pay, fringe benefits, job training, and classification, but they can include many other conditions, such as work location, days and times of work, and projects or tasks assigned.
(Public Law 88-352)	www.eeoc.gov/laws/statutes/titlevii.cfm
Pregnancy Discrimination Act of 1978, as amended	This amends Title VII of the Civil Rights Act of 1964 to prohibit discrimination on the basis of pregnancy, childbirth, or related medical conditions.
(Public Law 95-555)	www.eeoc.gov/laws/statutes/pregnancy.cfm
Equal Pay Act of 1963, as amended	This amends the Fair Labor Standards Act of 1938 to prohibit sex-based wage discrimination between men and women in the same establishment who perform jobs that require substantially equal skill, effort, and responsibility under similar working conditions.
(Public Law 88-38)	www.eeoc.gov/laws/statutes/epa.cfm
Age Discrimination in Employment Act of 1967, as amended	This prohibits employment discrimination based on age (40 and older) and prohibits employers from denying benefits to older employees. The Act first raised the mandatory retirement age and then was amended to eliminate it entirely for most occupations.
(Public Law 90-202)	www.eeoc.gov/laws/statutes/adea.cfm
Americans with Disabilities Act of 1990, as amended	Title I and Title V prohibit discrimination in aspects of employment against qualified individuals with disabilities and requires employers to make "reasonable accommodation." Other provisions of the Act ensure access to facilities, for example, libraries.
(Public Law 110-325)	www.ada.gov/pubs/ada.htm

Rehabilitation Act of 1973, as amended	Section 503 of the Act extends the requirements of the Americans with Disabilities Act to federal contractors and sub-contractors, and it requires employers to take affirmative action to employ and advance in employment qualified individuals with disabilities of all types. Most schools are federal contractors.
(Public Law 93-112)	www.dol.gov/compliance/laws/comp-rehab.htm
Genetic Information Nondiscrimination Act of 2008	Title II prohibits employment discrimination based on genetic information and places restrictions on employers' acquisition and disclosure of genetic information.
(Public Law 110-233)	www.eeoc.gov/laws/statutes/gina.cfm
Executive Order 11246 of 1965	This requires federal contractors to take affirmative action to ensure that all individuals have an equal opportunity for employment, without regard to race, color, religion, sex, national origin, disability, or status as a Vietnam era or special disabled veteran. The Order defines minorities as American Indian or Alaskan Native, Asian or Pacific Islander, Black, and Hispanic individuals. Most schools are federal contractors.
(EO 11246)	www.archives.gov/federal-register/codification/executive-order/11246.html
Uniformed Services Employment and Reemployment Rights Act of 1994, as amended	This ensures that persons who serve or have served in the Armed Forces, Reserves, National Guard, or other "uniformed services" are not disadvantaged in their civilian careers because of their service; are promptly reemployed in their civilian jobs upon their return from duty; and are not discriminated against in employment based on past, present, or future military service.
(Public Law 103-353)	www.dol.gov/vets/usc/vpl/usc38.htm
National Labor Relations Act of 1935, as amended	This guarantees the right to organize, form, join, or assist labor organizations and to bargain collectively. It restricts the actions employers may take to inhibit employees from organizing, bargaining collectively, or striking and other actions that would interfere with the right to organize. It applies only to portions of private sector employers. It established the National Labor Relations Board.
(Public Law 74-198)	www.law.cornell.edu/uscode/29/usc_sup_01_29_10_7_20_II.html

Executive Order 10988	This established the right of federal workers to engage in collective bargaining. It was superseded by Executive Order 11491.
(EO 10988)	www.archives.gov/federal-register/codification/executive-order/11491.html

Note: Links in the right column across from the PL or EO number lead to the full text of the legislation or order.

Key Federal Laws Protecting Employees' Health and Safety

Institutions have an interest in making sure their faculty and staff are healthy, safe, and secure in the workplace and when performing their jobs away from campus. Although the laws discussed in this section are designed to protect employees, they may be of greater interest to supervisors and administrators than to individual employees. Responsibility for complying with these laws is at the campus level, but it is useful for library personnel to have some familiarity with them. Along with one major federal law that established the employer's responsibility to provide a safe workplace for employees, there are guidelines for handling potentially toxic materials and state laws designed to care for and compensate workers injured on the job.

OCCUPATIONAL HEALTH AND SAFETY LAWS

The concept of employers taking responsibility to ensure the health and safety of their workers is a relatively new idea. Early in the twentieth century, the steel, mining, and railroad industries were criticized for ignoring workplace hazards, and organized labor began to push for safer working conditions. Insurance companies were starting to tie premiums to rates of injury and risks to occupations. In 1913, the National Safety Council was established to promote and educate the population about workplace safety, as well as about transportation and traffic safety. Early attempts at passing workers' compensation laws were declared unconstitutional by state courts, and not until 1916 did the U.S. Supreme Court declare workers' compensation constitutional. For the next 30 years, occupational safety was not a national priority, and little attention was paid to protecting workers. The major contribution to occupational safety during this period was the establishment of a national process to compile and analyze statistics on disabling injuries and deaths in the workplace. Unfortunately, reporting was voluntary on the part of employers, and only disabling injuries were counted. Little was known about occupational illnesses, and they were largely unreported.

In 1970 the Occupational Safety and Health Act (OSH Act) was passed, and it established the first national policy on workplace safety and health and the Occupational Safety and Health Administration (OSHA) to enforce standards, the National Institute for Occupational Safety and Health (NIOSH) to conduct and disseminate research on occupational health and safety, and the Occupational Safety and Health Review Commission (OSHRC) to adjudicate contested enforcement actions. The OSH Act empowered the Secretary of Labor to establish mandatory standards for health and safety and to issue guidelines that would apply to every workplace and for specialized, high-risk occupations. Some of the guidelines were developed for the construction, agriculture, medical and health care, and maritime industries, but the act includes the General Duty Clause stating that each employee has the right to "a place of employment which [is] free from recognized hazards that are causing or are likely to cause death or serious physical harm" (U.S. Code, 2012: 29 USC 654 5[a]([1]). Employees can refuse to work under conditions they believe to be unsafe and may not be punished for complaining to or filing a grievance with an employer, a union, OSHA, or any other government agency about job safety and health standards.

The most applicable and familiar set of OSHA guidelines in libraries might be those for emergency exit procedures, which were published in 1974. Also called "means of egress," the guidelines set standards to ensure that every employee could get from his or her work station to an outside door during a fire or other threatening condition and that emergency alarm systems were in place and working properly. The guidelines further require that every employer have a written workplace safety plan.

About half the U.S. states have taken responsibility for their own job safety and health management and have set standards that meet or exceed OSHA requirements. Many states and their counties have construction codes for safety, which add additional layers of specific requirements to public buildings, for example, for smoke exhaust systems, placement and installation of fire-rated doors, number and placement of fire extinguishers, emergency lighting, fire alarm systems (lights and horns), and so forth. OSHA does not cite employees for violations, only employers. However, OSHA does require employees "to comply with occupational safety and health standards and all rules, regulations, and orders issued pursuant to this Act which are applicable to his own actions and conduct" (U.S. Code, 2012: 29 USC 654 5[b]). Employees who refuse to comply with building evacuation procedures or, for example, continue to park book trucks in a hallway or otherwise obstruct a "means of egress," or refuse safety training, or prop open doors that are designed as fire-stop barriers may be subjected to legitimate disciplinary action. These requirements may be perceived by staff as aggravating, but, by ignoring them, they put themselves and others at risk.

WORKPLACE HAZARDS

Other areas of concern in library workplaces include the use of chemicals and cleaners, mold, and repetitive stress and musculoskeletal injuries. Libraries do not normally constitute hazardous workplaces requiring industry-specific regulations, so only those most applicable OSHA regulations and recommendations are discussed in this section.

Under the Hazard Communication regulation, OSHA requires that Materials Safety Data Sheets (MSDS) be made available to employees when potentially harmful substances are handled in the workplace. There are over 800 of these substances (www.osha.gov/SLTC/hazardoustoxic substances/index.html), but almost any substance can be considered toxic when not used as directed or intended. MSDS must be kept on file for substances as common as rubbing alcohol, and there may be additional state regulations specifying how much of the substance may be kept on hand. Manufacturers are responsible for developing MSDS for their products, and the National Library of Medicine maintains a searchable database of common household and office products by product name, ingredient, and health effect (http://householdproducts.nlm.nih.gov/index .htm). The database contains everything from hand soap, to cleaning products, to toner cartridges, and it can be useful in assisting employees to identify and avoid potential irritants or allergens they might encounter in the workplace.

Mold outbreak can be a periodic problem in libraries, especially in climates with high relative humidity, or in areas such as basements, where there may be inadequate air circulation and/or low lighting. However, there are no current federal standards or recommendations from OSHA, NIOSH, or the Environmental Protection Agency (EPA) as to permissible airborne concentrations of mold spores. Mold spores are ubiquitous and may present a hazard only when active, as in an outbreak when evidence is visible. Employers can be cited for violating the General Duty Clause of the OSH Act if there is a recognized hazard and reasonable steps are not taken to prevent or abate the hazard. OSHA does make recommendations for prevention and remediation, but these recommendations are informational only and employers are not cited for failing to take the recommendations contained in *A Brief Guide to Mold in the Workplace* (www .osha.gov/dts/shib/shib101003.html).

OSHA has not set standards for "sick building" syndrome, a term used to describe buildings in which occupants may experience acute discomfort, such as headache; eye, nose, or throat irritation; dry cough; dry or itchy skin; dizziness and nausea; difficulty in concentrating; fatigue; and sensitivity to odors. The symptoms are often relieved by leaving the building, but they may become chronic (e.g., higher rates of asthma have been attributed to sick building syndrome). The causes of sick building syndrome are unknown but usually have to do with poor indoor air quality, and they may include chemical or biological contaminants in building materials or contaminants entering the building from an outside source. OSHA does not have general standards for indoor air quality, but it does set standards for permissible levels of some airborne substances and for ventilation and air handling. The standards for airborne substances were developed largely for manufacturing environments rather than office environments, so even a careful building inspection may not reveal the source of the problem.

Musculoskeletal disorders (MSDs) are illnesses or injuries acquired over time and can be caused or exacerbated by repetitive motion, contact stress, or cumulative trauma to muscles, bones, connective tissue, or nerves. According to Assistant Secretary of Labor for Occupational Safety and Health, Dr. David Michaels, "Work-related musculoskeletal disorders remain the leading cause of workplace injury and illness in this country" (U.S. Department of Labor, OSHA, 2011b).

OSHA requires all workplace injuries to be recorded and reported, but the reporting requirement for MSDs has been intermittent during the past decade. In 2003 OSHA dropped MSDs from the injury reporting requirements and in 2011 withdrew a proposal to restore them in order to gather additional input from small businesses. However, OSHA states that it "will cite for ergonomic hazards under the General Duty Clause or issue ergonomic hazard letters [to employers] where appropriate as part of its overall enforcement program. OSHA encourages employers where necessary to implement effective programs or other measures to reduce ergonomic hazards and associated MSDs" but "will not focus its enforcement efforts on employers who are making good faith efforts to reduce ergonomic hazards" (U.S. Department of Labor, OSHA, 2011a). These statements could be taken to mean that OSHA will cite employers under the General Duty Clause if hazardous conditions are noticed during routine inspections and when employee(s) or unions have made specific complaints that are verified upon inspection. The exact causes and progress of MSDs in individuals can be a combination of poorly designed or inadequate equipment, harsh working conditions, and personal strength, posture, age, and work habits. Not all MSDs are work related (e.g., arthritis, gout, and fibromyalgia), but many MSDs can be aggravated by certain tasks or by the way tasks are performed, and workplace ergonomics can be applied to mitigate further injury and discomfort.

Technically, ergonomics is "the scientific discipline concerned with the understanding of interactions among humans and other elements of a system, and the profession that applies theory, principles, data, and other methods to design in order to optimize human well-being and overall system performance" (Human Factors and Ergonomics Society, 2012). The goal of ergonomics is to reduce stress and eliminate injuries and disorders associated with the overuse of muscles, bad posture, and repeated tasks. This involves designing tasks, work spaces, controls, displays, tools, lighting, and equipment to fit an employee's physical capabilities and limitations.

OSHA does offer recommendations for workplace ergonomics, and these are informational rather than regulatory. The recommendations are often industry specific (textiles, meatpacking, etc.), but the most applicable recommendations for libraries might be for computer workstation design, configuration, and use (www.osha.gov/SLTC/etools/computer workstations/more.html).

WORKERS' COMPENSATION

Despite efforts to maintain a safe workplace, accidents do happen, and they can happen inside or outside the regular workplace—walking across campus, attending conferences or workshops in other locations, or driving to alternate locations for work assignments. Workers' Compensation Insurance is a program designed to care for an employee injured on the job and to compensate employees who are unable to work due to the injury. Like other kinds of insurance, there is a premium for coverage, and the premium is paid by the employer, or the employer manages a pool of funds set aside to pay for medical care and lost wages. Although workers' compensation programs are federally regulated, they are operated by state governments and serve all employment sectors, with the exception of federal employees, who come under a different program operated by the federal government (see www.cutcomp.com/depts.htm for a state-by-state listing). The cost of insurance is determined by a state workers' compensation board, and the risk is spread across employees statewide rather than employees of a single employer. Each type of occupation is assigned a risk classification, and office workers have the lowest risk and therefore the lowest cost. Generally, workers' compensation programs make no attempt to assign blame. For example, if an employee falls down in the parking lot and is injured, blame is assigned neither to the employee (for perhaps wearing inappropriate shoes) nor to the employer (for a pothole in the parking lot surface). When an employee makes a claim and receives a monetary settlement for an injury, the employee relinquishes the right to sue the employer for negligence and, in some cases, to make future claims. Because of the number of situational variables and variations in individual state statutes, workers' compensation cases can be extremely complicated. The most important task for library administrators and supervisors is to see that injuries—on the job and wherever the job may take a staff member—are promptly reported. A phone call to the campus HR office, followed up with a completed injury report form, is the best practice.

This section discussed laws to protect employees from workplace harm, prevent illness in the workplace, and compensate employees for work-related injuries. Table 2.2 summarizes the major federal laws that protect employees' health and safety.

Table 2.2

KEY FEDERAL LAWS PROTECTING EMPLOYEES' HEALTH AND SAFETY

FEDERAL LAW	PURPOSE
Occupational Safety and Health Act of 1970, as amended	This establishes the right of employees to workplaces free from recognized hazards that are causing or are likely to cause death or serious physical harm. It requires employers to have a safety plan, to make information available about hazardous materials in the workplace, to record and report workplace injuries, and to permit safety inspections. It enables 1974 guidelines for "means of egress" to ensure the successful escape of employees in case of fire.
(Public Law 91-596)	www.osha.gov/pls/oshaweb/owadisp.show_document?p_table=OSHACT&p_id=2743
	About half the states have developed and operate their own OSHA-approved safety programs. For a listing, see www.osha.gov/dcsp/osp/faq.html#establishingyourown
	Emergency Exit Routes Fact Sheet www.osha.gov/OshDoc/data_General_Facts/emergency-exit-routes-factsheet.pdf
	Preventing Mold-Related Problems in the Indoor Workplace www.osha.gov/Publications/preventing_mold.pdf
Workers' Compensation National policy established by the Federal Workers' Compensation Act of 1916. States followed by creating their own governance agencies.	This is designed to care for an employee injured on the job and to compensate employees who are unable to work because of the injury for their losses. *Workers' Compensation Contacts by State* www.dol.gov/owcp/dfec/regs/compliance/wc.htm *Advanced Insurance Management, a commercial consulting firm, provides state-by-state information, with links to important regulatory agencies* www.cutcomp.com/depts.htm

Note: Links in the right column across from the PL number lead to the full text of the legislation or order. Additional links go to useful guidelines or information by state.

Key Federal Laws Protecting Employees' Job Rights and Access to Health Care

Along with laws to protect employees from harm, to prevent illness in the workplace, and to compensate employees for work-related injuries, there are laws to protect a person's job while the person is absent due to extended personal or family illness and to continue health insurance at group cost after employees have separated from the organization. Because these laws are administered at the campus level, only a general overview is provided. A benefits counselor at the campus HR office can help answer complex questions about individual situations.

HEALTH INSURANCE AND INSURANCE CONTINUATION

The uncertainties surrounding the passage of the Patient Protection and Affordable Care Act of 2010 have left many employers and employees, including those in colleges and universities, somewhat unsure of the exact terms of health care reform. At present, there is no federal law requiring an employer to pay part or all of the cost of individual or family health insurance for its employees, nor would the legislation of 2010 require an employer to do so. This is a benefit offered by employers—a noncash form of compensation—rather than a legal entitlement. Health care reform legislation requires employers who meet certain criteria to offer affordable health care coverage either through a cooperative or a medical insurance provider, but it would not require them to pay the cost. Both employers and individuals who "opt out" of the insurance requirement would pay a penalty. The legislation also extends adult children's eligibility for coverage on their parents' health plans, ends the practice of capping or limiting a person's lifetime covered medical expenses, and prohibits coverage exclusions for preexisting conditions.

Fortunately for library administrators, staff compensation and benefits are administered by the campus HR division. Questions and problems should be directed to the benefits specialist within the campus HR division. If a union has negotiated health insurance coverage on behalf of its members, then the employer must make good on its contractual promise to employees. Assuming health insurance coverage is a staff benefit offered by all colleges and universities, there is a federal law mandating the extension of insurance benefits after an employee separates from the employer or loses benefit status for life events such as the death of the employed spouse, divorce from the employed spouse, during unemployment between jobs, or due to the reduction in the number of hours worked. The requirement to offer continued health coverage is most often called COBRA, referring to broader legislation that contains the provision for coverage—the Consolidated Omnibus Budget Reconciliation Act of 1985. Eligible persons are ensured the continuing availability of identical health coverage at no more than 102 percent of the employer's cost and may continue coverage for a period of time between 18 and 36 months depending on individual circumstances. The affected person must pay for coverage, but the premium is typically far less than it would be for an individual seeking coverage on the open market. For a short period of time, the COBRA benefit offered reduced premiums to those who were laid off during a period of economic recession, but the enabling legislation has expired, and the reduction does not apply to those laid off on or after May 31, 2010.

FAMILY MEDICAL LEAVE

One of the most familiar and most used job protections is family medical leave. The Family Medical Leave Act of 1993 (FMLA) requires employers to provide unpaid, job-protected leave for up to 12 weeks for an employee to care for his or her own serious health challenge or that of a spouse, child, or parent. The act has since been amended to extend the 12 weeks of protected leave for members of military families to address obligations related to the family member's service, such as attending military events, arranging for alternative child care, attending counseling sessions, and taking care of legal and financial arrangements. The leave period is extended to 26 weeks for employees who need to care for a related service member who has been injured or become ill during active duty. Family medical leave can be taken as straight time (any number of consecutive workdays or workweeks up to the limit), or intermittently (two afternoons a week, for example), or as a reduction in hours worked (working 20 hours a week, for example), depending on medical necessity.

In order to qualify for FMLA benefits, an employee must have worked for at least one year and must have worked at least 1,250 hours (approximately half-time) during the previous 12 months. Qualifying family members include only spouses, children, and parents, and, in the case of military entitlements, the service member's next of kin. Family medical leave is available to men as well as women for childbirth or adoption or in their other roles as family caregivers. Employers may create, but are not required to create, compassionate policies to extend FMLA benefits to relationships other than immediate family members, for example, to employees for their domestic partners or to employees for less immediate family members for whom they are the sole responsible caregiver or the next of kin. Employers may also offer paid FMLA leave but are not required to do so.

An employer must maintain health coverage for the employee during the unpaid family medical leave leave period and restore the employee to the same or an equivalent position with equivalent pay and benefits when the employee returns to work. No loss of previously accrued benefits can result from the use of family medical leave, and employers may not punish or discriminate against an employee for using or attempting to use family medical leave benefits.

When foreseeable, employees must provide 30 days' advance notice when requesting family medical leave or notify the employer as soon as it is practical do so. When possible, employees must make reasonable efforts to schedule leave so as not to disrupt the employer's operations. In order to assist with the leave certification or qualification process, employees have a responsibility to provide sufficient information and to communicate with the employer. "Sufficient information" may include a doctor's or other health care provider's letter or signed statement, the estimated duration of the expected leave, and whether or not the request is for the same reason that previous FMLA leave has been taken. Periodically, employees may be required to recertify or reverify the continuing need for leave. It is to the employee's advantage to assist in the qualification process and communicate with HR personnel, both in the library and on the campus, throughout the period of need. FMLA records may help to establish the beginning date of a disability or support claims for other types of benefits. Employers may, and often do, require employees to expend all other applicable paid leave prior to requesting family medical leave, and this policy can protect an employee from future harm. It is very important to keep those facing the most serious health challenges insured for as long as possible. Once FMLA leave has been exhausted, the employee may be required to pay the cost of continued health coverage, and this happens just when the employee needs health insurance the most but is the least able to pay for it. To be practical, this is another good reason employees should take care to manage their paid sick or personal leave days. Taking them for reasons other than illness or because they are "there for the taking" can disadvantage an employee in the future.

Table 2.3 summarizes the major laws to protect employees' jobs rights and access to health care.

Table 2.3

KEY FEDERAL LAWS PROTECTING EMPLOYEES' JOB RIGHTS AND ACCESS TO HEALTH CARE

FEDERAL LAW	PURPOSE
Patient Protection and Affordable Care Act of 2010	This amends a number of existing federal laws and creates a new law to improve the quality, efficiency, and affordability of health care for all Americans. It extends adult children's eligibility for coverage on their parents' health plans, ends the practice of capping or limiting a person's lifetime covered medical expenses, and prohibits coverage exclusions for preexisting conditions.
(Public Law 111–148)	**www.gpo.gov/fdsys/pkg/PLAW-111publ148/pdf/ PLAW-111publ148.pdf** *Understanding the Affordable Care Act: About the Law* **www.healthcare.gov/law/about/index.html**
Consolidated Omnibus Budget Reconciliation Act of 1985, as amended Continuation of Health Care Benefits Coverage	This requires employers to offer unpaid continuation of health insurance to employees at the time of separation from employment. Coverage may cost no more than 102 percent of employer's premium, must be identical to coverage of existing employees, and must be made available for not less than 18 months.
(Public Law 99-272)	**www.ssa.gov/OP_Home/comp2/F099-272.html** *Facts for Employees About COBRA* **www.dol.gov/ebsa/faqs/faq_consumer_cobra.HTML**
Family Medical Leave Act of 1993, as amended	This protects certain job rights of employees to take extended unpaid leave for one's own injury, illness, pregnancy, childbirth, or adoption and to care for an immediate family member who faces a health challenge. It applies equally, regardless of gender. It extends benefits for military families to meet special obligations.
(Public Law 103-3)	**www.dol.gov/whd/fmla/fmlaAmended.htm** *Fact Sheet on FMLA* **www.dol.gov/whd/regs/compliance/whdfs28.htm**

Note: Links in the right column across from the PL number lead to the full text of the legislation or order. Additional links go to useful guidelines.

As well as laws to protect a person's job while absent due to extended personal or family illness and to continue health insurance at group cost after employees have separated from the organization, there are other laws that protect the privacy of personal information and control what employers may ask, when they may ask, and how they may use personal information about a person's health, physical and mental abilities, finances, and criminal background.

Key Federal Laws Protecting Employees' Private Information

There are federal protections for employees governing how an employer is permitted to obtain personal information about a present or future employee and how the information may be used. These laws offer what might be less protection than academic and library employees would expect, but, nonetheless, they regulate the use of potential or existing employees' personal information of various types, including criminal background and credit checks and the use of controlled substances. These laws change along with societal attitudes and deal with issues that affect the privacy of individuals' personal information.

Attitudes toward the use of employment prescreening tools to obtain credit histories and criminal records appear to be changing, and federal and state laws are currently in question. Some states have begun to prohibit the practice of asking job applicants about criminal records on initial application forms, to limit the use of credit histories to high-risk positions, and to make hiring decisions in general. There is an ongoing national policy discussion about the accuracy of available information and the effectiveness of background screening practices, as well as the general fairness of using past behavior to predict future behavior. These practices may adversely impact women, minorities, or those with health challenges (Roberts, 2011).

BACKGROUND AND CREDIT CHECKS

Title III of the Consumer Credit Protection Act of 1968 provides that an employee may not be dismissed because of legal garnishment for a single debt. "Garnishment" is the act of withholding part of a person's paycheck and turning it over to the agency that is owed money or that represents an entity who is owed money, for example, the Internal Revenue Service, the U.S. Department of Education, or a student loan guarantor. For positions of trust (jobs that involve handling money or other assets of the institution, such as credit card purchasing or processing credit card payments), candidates may be asked to submit to credit checks prior to hire. There is no federal law that prevents an employer from performing credit checks prior to employment (in addition to other background checks). However, there may be state laws regulating or prohibiting these practices. Criminal background checks are permissible, and some colleges and universities perform them on all employees at hire, some on no employees, and some on only employees who work with children.

Two provisions of the Fair Credit Reporting Act of 1970 apply to the manner in which employers can obtain information about applicants' credit histories. One provision restrains consumer reporting agencies from providing information about employees' or applicants' credit histories without the individual's written consent, and another requires employers who have declined to hire an applicant, or taken adverse action against an employee, to notify an individual of the action and provide contact information for the source of the report. The Fair Credit Reporting Act of 1970 is enforced by the U.S. Federal Trade Commission.

DRUG-FREE WORKPLACE ACT OF 1988
This act is a subtitle of larger legislation, the Anti-Drug Abuse Act of 1988, and requires employers to maintain a drug-free workplace by establishing and communicating a policy that explicitly prohibits the manufacture, use, or distribution of controlled substances in the workplace and that describes what actions will be taken in the event of violations. Although not required, many colleges and universities ask employees to sign statements acknowledging that they have been informed of the policy at the point of hire. Such signed statements are used to verify that the employer has communicated the policy. The act permits, but does not mandate, employee drug screening or testing or require the creation of programs for counseling or rehabilitation.

ADA ESSENTIAL FUNCTIONS, MEDICAL EXAMS, AND GENETIC INFORMATION
Along with employment protections discussed earlier in this chapter, the ADA also protects job applicants from what might be considered

unnecessary probes about their ability or inability to perform the tasks of a job, and from employers collecting more information than might actually be needed to determine if a reasonable accommodation is required. Although most colleges and universities do not ask potential employees to undergo medical examinations, they would be permitted to do so if there were a business necessity. For example, it would not be impossible to imagine requesting a potential chancellor or president to undergo a medical examination. It could be reasonable to assume that the job requires extraordinary stamina, would involve frequent travel, and would normally be stressful. However, such a medical examination may be requested *only* after an offer has been made. The results could be used to determine whether the individual could perform the essential functions of the job. Far more typical is the use of an ADA "checklist," or essential functions checklist, which describes the physical or mental tasks required to perform a job. Such checklists include activities such as standing, sitting, or reading a computer screen for sustained periods of time; climbing stairs, pushing, bending, stooping; and understanding written directions. Employers may request a candidate to indicate that he or she can perform such tasks, with or without reasonable accommodation, but *only* after an offer has been made. The principle here is to avoid discrimination while at the same time ensuring that the candidate is informed of the physical and mental tasks that will be required and has an opportunity to request an accommodation. Activities on the checklist *must* be job related and require some degree of regular performance; that is, they would be a hardship to delegate to another employee.

The Genetic Information Nondiscrimination Act (GINA) of 2008 prohibits any employment practice that affects any aspect of employment based on an individual's genetic history and strictly limits the conditions under which an employer may request, require, purchase, or otherwise obtain an individual's genetic information. The most likely application permitted by this law in a library setting would be when an employer requests the information in order to assist an employee in meeting the certification requirements for FMLA leave eligibility. Even in this instance, prior written consent of the employee is required. In brief, Table 2.4 summarizes the major applicable laws regarding the privacy of personal information and their purposes.

Table 2.4

KEY FEDERAL LAWS PROTECTING EMPLOYEES' PRIVATE INFORMATION

FEDERAL LAW	PURPOSE
Consumer Credit Protection Act of 1968, as amended	This provides that an employee cannot be dismissed because of a legal garnishment for a single debt.
(Public Law 90-321)	www.fdic.gov/regulations/laws/rules/6500-200.html
Fair Credit Reporting Act of 1970, as amended	This prohibits consumer reporting agencies from providing information about employees' or applicants' credit histories without the individual's written consent, and it requires employers who have declined to hire an applicant, or taken adverse action against an employee, to notify an individual of the action and to provide contact information for the source of the report.
(Public Law 91-508)	www.ftc.gov/os/statutes/031224fcra.pdf *A Summary of Your Rights* www.ftc.gov/bcp/edu/pubs/consumer/credit/cre35.pdf
Drug-Free Workplace Act of 1988, as amended	This requires employers to maintain a drug-free workplace by establishing and communicating a policy that explicitly prohibits the manufacture, use, or distribution of controlled substances in the workplace and what actions will be taken in the event of violations. Alcohol is not a controlled substance for the purposes of the Act, and the Act does not require employee drug testing.
(Public Law 100-690)	www.dol.gov/elaws/asp/drugfree/require.htm *Frequently Asked Questions* www.dol.gov/elaws/asp/drugfree/screenfq.htm
Americans with Disabilities Act of 1990, as amended	This outlines information that can be collected from employees at hire regarding their ability to perform certain tasks, and it describes what constitutes reasonable accommodations.
(Public Law 110-325)	www.ada.gov/pubs/ada.htm *Reasonable Accommodation Workplace Guidelines* www.eeoc.gov/policy/docs/accommodation.html

Genetic Information Nondiscrimination Act of 2008	This prohibits an employer from discriminating against employees or applicants based on their genetic history and severely limits the circumstances under which an employer may ask for or possess such information.
Public Law 110–233	www.eeoc.gov/laws/statutes/gina.cfm
	Frequently Asked Questions www.genome.gov/10002328

Note: Links in the right column across from the PL number lead to the full text of the legislation or order. Additional links go to useful guidelines.

Summary

There are numerous federal laws that protect basic employment rights, and these apply to everyone from the library director or dean to the student worker. Everyone has the right to equal opportunity, to a workplace that is safe and free of hazard, to compassionate benefits when facing illness or family needs, and to protection against unnecessary probes into private information. However, no federal or state law or regulatory requirement can fix hostile relationships among library staff members or between staff members and supervisors. The next chapters deal with interpersonal relationships in the workplace at the coworker and supervisory levels.

REFERENCES

American Rights at Work. 2008. "The Haves and the Have-Nots: How American Labor Law Denies a Quarter of the Workforce Collective Bargaining Rights." American Rights at Work Organization. November. www.americanrights atwork.org/publications/general/the-haves-and-have-nots-20081121 -680-92-92.html.

Applegate, Rachel. 2009. "Who Benefits? Unionization and Academic Libraries and Librarians." *Library Quarterly* 79, no. 4: 443–463.

Association for College and Research Libraries. 2008. "Guideline on Collective Bargaining." American Library Association. June. www.ala.org/ala/mgrps/ divs/acrl/standards/guidelinecollective.cfm.

Human Factors and Ergonomics Society. 2012. "What Is Human Factors/Ergonomics?" Human Factors and Ergonomics Society. Accessed May 15. www.hfes.org/web/AboutHFES/about.html.

McCook, Kathleen de la Peña. 2009. "Unions in Public and Academic Libraries." In *Encyclopedia of Library and Information Sciences,* edited by Marcia J. Bates and Mary Niles Maack. 3rd ed. Vol. 1: 1, 5337–5346. Boca Raton, FL: CRC Press.

National Center for Collective Bargaining in Higher Education and the Professions. 2006. "Brief Summary of Results." In *Directory of Faculty Contracts and Bargaining Agents in Higher Education.* New York: Hunter College, City University of New York. www.hunter.cuny.edu/ncscbhep/assets/files/summary _directory.doc.

National Gay and Lesbian Taskforce. 2009. "Nondiscrimination Laws Map." National Gay and Lesbian Taskforce. Last modified July 1. www.thetaskforce .org/reports_and_research/nondiscrimination_laws.

Roberts, Bill. 2011. "Close-Up on Screening." *HR Magazine* 56, no. 2: 22–29.

Segal, Jonathan A. 2010. "A Guide for Managers to Protected Groups." *Bloomberg Businessweek,* April 16. www.businessweek.com/managing/content/apr2010/ca20100415_757558.htm.

U.S. Code. 2012. Title 29: The Occupational Safety and Health Act of 1970. Section 5. Duties (a)(1) and (b). Accessed May 15. www.osha.gov/pls/oshaweb/owadisp.show_document?p_table=OSHACT&p_id=3359.

U.S. Congress, House. 2009. Employment Non-Discrimination Act, H.R. 2981, 111th Congress. Civic Impulse, LLC. www.govtrack.us/congress.

U.S. Department of Labor, Bureau of Labor Statistics. 2012. "Union Members Summary." Last modified January 27. U.S. Department of Labor. www.bls.gov/news.release/union2.nr0.htm.

U.S. Department of Labor, Occupational Safety and Health Administration. 2011a. "Ergonomics Enforcement." U.S. Department of Labor. Accessed March 5. www.osha.gov/SLTC/ergonomics/faqs.html.

———. 2011b. "U.S. Labor Department's OSHA Temporarily Withdraws Proposed Column for Work-Related Musculoskeletal Disorders, Reaches Out to Small Businesses." January 25. www.osha.gov/pls/oshaweb/owadisp.show_document?p_table=NEWS_RELEASES&p_id=19158.

U.S. Government Printing Office. 2011. "Title 29: Labor §31.2(1)(i)." In *Code of Federal Regulations.* Washington, DC: U.S. Government Printing Office. http:// ecfr.gpoaccess.gov.

working with others

There are few jobs that can be done in complete isolation in libraries. Perhaps some tasks of a job are autonomous, but the entire span of a person's responsibilities always impacts or dovetails with the work of others. Everyone depends to some degree on others to accomplish work, and most are collocated with one or more persons in their work areas or at a service point. Whether they are work partners, a work group, or desk neighbors, social and task interaction with coworkers is inevitable. In library organizations, all work is interdependent and coworkers form a human ecosystem in which everyone is someone's coworker. The potential for both coworker support and coworker antagonism is high. The stress of constant change in highly interdependent organizations can create "perfect storm" conditions for interpersonal conflict. On the other hand, coworkers have a unique potential to provide work-related and social support to one another that improves productivity and decision making and adds richness to the work experience. Although supervisors and human resource (HR) professionals can intervene in situations when conflict gets out of hand and begins to distract or disrupt the larger working group, the best cure is prevention at the individual level. Harassment, which is against the law, and bullying are specialized workplace hazards and require organizational assistance to remediate.

Foundation and Philosophy

Most management texts identify the earliest research on the behavior of people working in groups as the "Hawthorne Experiments." These were a series of studies conducted during a five-year period (1927–1932) in a factory environment, the Western Electric Hawthorne Works in Chicago. The early Hawthorne studies examined the relationship between working conditions (lighting, temperature and humidity levels, break periods, working hours) and productivity. However, the most celebrated findings came later, at the end of the series of experiments, when researchers withdrew control of working conditions from the workers and, to their surprise, productivity continued to increase. After much analysis, the researchers determined that the most significant factor in increasing productivity had been the creation of a sense of group identity and the increased social support and cohesion that came with increased worker interaction. Among their specific findings, Elton Mayo (1945) found that the relationship between the supervisor and work group affected productivity, as did work group norms, and that the workplace had a distinct culture, and simply belonging to a group acted as a reward for many people. The increase in productivity that accompanies a person's sense of belonging to a group of caring coworkers is called the "Hawthorne Effect." Mayo's work established the idea of grouping employees into work teams, a practice followed to this day, and he is credited as the father of the "human relations school" of management *("Human Relations School," 2001)*. These ideas may seem obvious to us now, but Mayo "discovered" the enormous importance of coworker relationships.

Influences of Coworkers

Coworkers are narrowly defined as those who have lateral relationships—one's peers rather than those above or below in the organizational hierarchy. Coworkers have a great deal of influence on one another as individuals and on the work group, including the power to support or antagonize one other. Typical supportive actions include offering to help accomplish a large or difficult task, offering to teach a new skill and coach during the skill development period, stepping in to cover during a coworker's absence or schedule conflict, showing a new coworker "the ropes," and exhibiting general friendliness or positive affect. These behaviors engender a work environment that is pleasant, welcoming, and inclusive. Antagonistic actions include undesirable behaviors such as subverting or sabotaging group efforts, demeaning or ridiculing others, complaining more than the norm, and incivility. These behaviors engender a work environment that is uncomfortable, exclusive, and hostile. Supportive and antagonistic behaviors are linked to important individual employee outcomes, such as having a clear and accurate role perception and positive work attitude, levels of engagement or withdrawal, general effectiveness, and job satisfaction.

Although much can be assumed about a work group from its collective relationship with the supervisor, and in terms of productivity, effectiveness, and job satisfaction, it is true that the supervisor has a great influence on group culture—in reducing conflict, setting the tone for how people treat one another, modeling appropriate professional behavior, and motivating the group. However, many studies since the Hawthorne Experiments have concluded that coworkers have an influence separate and distinct from that of the supervisor or higher leaders. Coworker support has been found to be a greater predictor than leadership support in terms of job engagement/withdrawal, effort reduction (slacking off), and attendance/absenteeism (Chiaburu and Harrison, 2008).

Coworkers spend more time with one another than with a supervisor or other leaders, and there is less social distance among coworkers. Coworkers may be more forthright with one another because the interpersonal risk is perceived as lower and because shared responsibility and equal organizational status tend to encourage stronger affiliations. In contrast to the supervisor, whose job in part is to encourage and motivate supervisees by recognizing their contributions, coworkers have no such obligation, and their comments, both positive and negative, may have more credibility because they are given freely. This is true across all horizontal levels of an organization. Coworkers have the power to set group norms for productivity, to define the boundaries for appropriate and inappropriate behaviors, and to negotiate a shared culture.

COWORKER SUPPORT AND COHESION

Many positive individual and organizational benefits have been attributed to coworker support. In a meta-analysis of previous research on the topic, Chiaburu and Harrison (2008) found that in addition to increasing worker engagement and productivity, there was also cumulative evidence that coworker social support was related to lowering individual stress levels, reducing burnout, and reducing physical strain. Another study, reported by Dittman (2003) in the American Psychological Association's *Monitor on Psychology*, found that employees who seek social support at work—especially during high-stress moments—may lower their blood pressure and improve their cardiovascular health. There is considerable evidence for a long list of positive effects promoted by supportive coworker relationships.

Support behaviors can be divided into two categories—social support and instrumental support. Social support behaviors include showing empathy, caring, and general friendliness. They bond coworkers together through conversations about non-work-related events, confiding and listening to one another's problems, and providing emotional and spiritual support during difficult times. Instrumental support behaviors include sharing information about the organization, a work process, or a task at hand; offering advice or feedback on the quality of performance; teaching, coaching, or mentoring; as well as offering to assist directly with work or offering to share tools or other resources. Social support is thought to be an important influence on employees' attitudes toward work but not especially influential in terms of employee effectiveness. Instrumental support, on the other hand, tends to improve job performance and productivity. It can have beneficial effects on one's perception of his or her individual job role; that is, the supporting individual can provide cues or direct advice to reduce the tension of ambiguity about the job or the organization and help the individual better define and understand his or her role. It can help with role overload by assisting an individual in sorting out priorities and discriminating between activities that are genuinely important and those that are merely routine. It is human nature to expect that supportive behaviors will be reciprocated, and support is usually offered on the assumption (conscious or unconscious) that cooperation will be returned in the future. In fact, if such cooperation is not reciprocated between interdependent peers, then it may lead to competitive behaviors, such as hoarding resources or information.

This is not to say that librarians are stingy; in fact, the profession tends to attract those whose passion is service to others. However, the expectation of reciprocity does offer some explanation why cooperation may not always be an attractive prospect. Reciprocity requires some length of time in which the supporter can "collect" and the ability of the supported to return a favor in-kind. An employee anticipating retirement may not be interested in providing instrumental support to others because the time line required for reciprocity is too short. Colleagues outside the home department or outside the library may not feel they have a legitimate expectation of reciprocity and therefore don't feel compelled to provide instrumental support. How many times have librarians tried to get teaching faculty to cooperate on a project, or fill out surveys, or participate in focus groups only to be rebuffed? It is very hard to ask for instrumental support without the ability to provide reciprocal and in-kind instrumental support.

Social support, on the other hand, is considered to rise in importance between and among coworkers as the social intensity of the work rises. For example, when work involves direct contact with patrons at a busy service desk, social support for coworkers—expressions of empathy, general friendliness, and personal caring—can greatly improve attitudes toward work, job satisfaction, and cohesion among members of the work group. Strong coworker affiliation can directly affect the delivery of service. Coworkers consciously or unconsciously teach one another how finely policies should be interpreted, when exceptions can be made, how much blame can be assigned or not assigned to other groups or to the adequacy of their tools, and how a myriad of other small and subjective judgments should be made. Whether or not these judgments are correct, strongly cohesive coworkers will adopt a consistent approach to them because the value of affiliation is considered greater than the value of correctness. The power of a congenial workplace where coworkers have friendly relationships should not be underestimated. The longer people work together, the more intimate information they may share, and the more likely they are to shape one another's opinions and behaviors. In fact, there is evidence to believe that social ties (friendship networks) in the workplace may be stronger than instrumental ties (helping and advice networks), especially during periods of organizational change (Krackhardt, 1992).

"Best friends at work" has become a fairly common phenomenon in the past few years. Based in part on Gallup Surveys, Rath (2006) maintains that people who have a best friend at work are seven times more likely to be highly engaged and experience greater job satisfaction, and they are less likely to leave their jobs. Undoubtedly, having social support at work can enhance the job experience and helps during periods of overwork (implementing new software, building renovation and/or moving work locations), or workload creep (three people now doing the work of five), or during foundational change in the work environment (closing departments or branches), but the "best friends" dyad is loaded with toxic potential. If one friend expects the other to cover for errors or reduced efforts, or one friend is promoted or transferred, or socializing replaces

Are there any regulations that prohibit workplace romance?

The risks and benefits of being best friends at work also extend to coworkers who become romantically involved. Like friendship, romance is virtually impossible to regulate, but it introduces additional issues of employee privacy, the perception of fair treatment, and potential claims of sexual harassment. These side issues automatically involve the employer. Because the employer does not normally have a legal right to control lawful personal behaviors outside work, they would not be permitted to inquire about such relationships. If one member of a couple wishes to leave the relationship but the other continues pursuit in the workplace, this could be possible grounds for a claim of sexual harassment, and the employer would have to respond. If the couple is perceived as having special privileges, for example, always permitted to schedule time off concurrently for vacations, excused for taking the occasional long lunch hour together, allowing displays of affection or hostility that are disruptive or annoying to others to go unchecked, or the couple appears to exert an undue influence in workplace matters, then the general perception may be that others are not being treated fairly. Most public employers prohibit nepotism (being in a position to influence any aspect of employment for a relative, including a spouse), and most prohibit faculty involvement in romantic relationships with students, but few prohibit romantic relationships between adult peers because such prohibitions are not realistically enforceable. Like the best friend relationship, the onus is on the involved couple to behave professionally in the workplace during and after the relationship and to show respect and consideration for others.

getting the work done, then the entire work group begins to suffer. If the level of intimacy is too intense, or too much personal information has been shared, the boundary between work life and personal life may be crossed and the relationship sullied in both arenas. The risk of best friend "backfire" can be high, and, when these relationships turn toxic, they can result in especially ugly situations. An event in or out of the workplace that is considered a personal betrayal can turn best friends into enemies, and the drama inevitably unfolds in the workplace.

CONFLICT BETWEEN COWORKERS

Undoubtedly, there are library working environments characterized by interpersonal conflict between two coworkers or among a group of coworkers. Unless someone is a perfect human being, at some time he or she has played an active role in one unnecessary conflict or another. Disagreements over what might be seen as very small things—the font or colors used on a webpage, the type of coffee to make in the morning, or who should or shouldn't have to clean the microwave—can quickly escalate into war.

If it seems libraries are too often dens of conflict, there are good reasons—the organic and interconnected nature of work in libraries, the relentless pace of change, and the increasing scarcity of resources. For many years, women have dominated the student ranks of library schools, and, although less so than other types of libraries, academic libraries still tend to be staffed by more women than men and even more so in the paraprofessional ranks. The predominance of women in academic libraries can affect the nature of conflict and the ways in which interpersonal conflict is addressed or, more likely, avoided. The general theory is that overt female aggression is met with social disapproval, and women are socialized during their early years to avoid conflict. Women may have been taught that they are not allowed to brag or talk about their accomplishments. More often, they are taught to play down, or even deny, that their achievements were due to anything but luck. This socialization is in opposition to the reality of the work environment, where status, pay, and opportunity are judged and awarded based on individual performance. The conflict between how women have been taught to behave and a political workplace where perception is often treated as fact can leave women to resolve the dissonance by becoming indirect communicators. Indirect communication styles rely more on context and body language for meaning than the exact words spoken or written, for example, the subtle put-down or backhanded compliment, the withering stare, exclusion of a coworker from lunch invitations, and so forth. A precise understanding of the delicacies of context could be requisite for membership in a clique. Clique members are simply easier to communicate with and are less likely to press for direct communication. This accounts for some difficulty on the part of a supervisor to understand the exact nature of conflicts or disputes when they rest more on context than on overt behavior. Some women (and men) find the dissonance between their socialization and their working environment so uncomfortable that they compensate by being overly aggressive or may swing wildly between aggression and syrupy sweetness.

Regardless of gender and communication styles, there are very few, if any, library jobs that do not rely on the work of others in order to accomplish goals, and all library jobs impact other jobs in the library. The culture of higher education is based on challenging ideas and theories, and academics cast a critical eye on almost everything. This is also true of librarians and other library professionals. In contrast to this willingness to examine concepts and ideas, librarians may come to a library with, or later develop, a firm set of deeply held beliefs about the nature of librarianship, and these beliefs may not be as open to challenge as intellectual concepts or ideas. To challenge a person's deeply held beliefs is to challenge the person, and this is far more threatening than challenging a person's ideas about process or how things should be done. This can be a difficult line to walk, particularly in higher education. In preparation for writing a book on conflict management, Montgomery and Cook (2005) asked librarians of all types to respond to structured questions about their libraries' organizational climate, conflict, and conflict management. The authors were overwhelmed to receive 500 responses, and it is clear they touched a nerve. The volume of detailed responses, many including personal accounts of conflict engagements, should be enough to verify that libraries are hardly safe havens or places to escape strife.

Despite confirmation that we are all human and all subject to conflict, there is an expectation of all library staff, faculty or not, to observe the principles of collegiality. Collegiality has to do with being a team player, as well as being respectful to coworkers. A "college" is a group of professionals joined by a common purpose, and collegiality is the respect each person has for the other's commitment to that common purpose. It is an important concept in organizations where independence of thought, innovation, and interdisciplinarity are essential to success. Mutual respect for coworkers becomes the primary social control for avoiding the damaging aspects of conflict. Northern Illinois University (2011) explains the concept in a written collegiality policy, which states in part:

> Collegiality is not congeniality nor is it conformity or excessive deference to the judgments of colleagues, supervisors and administrators; these are flatly oppositional to the free and open development of ideas. Evidence of collegiality is demonstrated by the protection of academic freedom, the capacity of colleagues to carry out their professional functions without obstruction, and the ability of a community of scholars to thrive in a vigorous and collaborative intellectual climate.

In very simple terms, the basic principles of collegiality are intellectual respect and consideration for others and must be observed even in the most extreme or heated situations. The American Library Association's Code of Ethics prescribes that "We treat co-workers and other colleagues with respect, fairness, and good faith, and advocate conditions of employment that safeguard the rights and welfare of all employees of our institutions" (American Library Association, 2008). Making a request ("I'd appreciate it if you would . . .") rather than a demand ("Before you leave today, I want you to . . .") sends a message of asking for assistance rather than expecting obeisance. Conducting oneself in a professional manner by avoiding gossip circles; refusing to comment on another's dress, speech, appearance, or beliefs; allowing others to save face even at the cost of your own; and being tolerant of opposing opinions can all create social capital with colleagues. Trust takes a long time to earn, but it can disappear instantly because of a single thoughtless mistake.

Managing Conflict

The textbook definition of interpersonal conflict requires three conditions: there must be an expressed struggle; the struggle must be between at least two parties who are interdependent; and the parties must believe one or more of the parties are interfering with the other(s) reaching their goals (Wilmot and Hocker, 2007). The conflict must be expressed—observable in behaviors or expressions that are aggressive, angry, argumentative, harsh, or intended to demean or ridicule another. Those involved in the conflict are interdependent—neither party believes that his or her desired goals can be achieved without the support, assistance, or agreement of the other party. Both parties believe that the other is standing in the way of goal achievement. Whether or not this is an accurate belief has no bearing. It is the perception of a barrier that creates initial conflict. If the parties have no dependence on one another or no interaction at all, then there can be no conflict.

GROUP CONFLICT

Once the conditions required for conflict (interdependency, hostility, and the perception of goal blocking) are met, the level of conflict can be analyzed. There are situational factors affecting the level and intensity of conflict, and these include the degree of interdependency among the parties, the number of parties involved, the urgency of one or both parties' needs, and whether the parties believe they represent an important constituency. If one or more of the parties have a history of conflict, together or separately, conflict can be exacerbated by grudges or simply be the learned behavioral response to any perception of threat, even if the goal is perceived as relatively insignificant:

- If the degree of interdependence is high, for example, between the acquisitions function and the cataloging function, or between the public services function and the webmaster or web maintenance group, the potential for conflict is increased.
- If the conflict is librarywide, for example between library administration and unit or department heads over strategic direction, then it involves many actors and high stakes, and the potential for conflict is increased.
- Whatever the expressed conflict may be, if the consequences are perceived as extreme, such as an act of violence or irreparable harm will occur if the goal is not met, then the urgency of finding a solution can elevate the potential for conflict.
- If one or more of the parties believe they represent an important constituency and are responsible for achieving the constituency's

desired goal, then the potential for conflict can increase. For example, staff in public service units may take responsibility for seeing that patrons' needs are met and believe that meeting these needs should be the library's first priority. Library administrators represent the provost and the academic concerns of the institution and believe they are responsible to the greater organization for goal achievement. Certainly, these beliefs are not unreasonable, but they increase the potential for conflict. One group may attempt to escape its shared responsibility for resolving the conflict and solve the problem by imposing power.

- If one or more of the parties have a history of shared conflict, they may begin to keep score in terms of "wins" and "losses," carry grudges, or consider one another "enemies." These are the most extreme situations and arise when conflict has been ignored for long periods of time. At this point, hostile behaviors are so well developed as a response pattern that the potential for conflict is high all the time.

Estimating the situational factors can assist in developing resolution strategies for group conflict, but reaching a resolution requires patience, time, and, perhaps, assistance from a third party. Conflicts that involve situational variables can be difficult to resolve, and the greater the number of situational variables involved, the more time it may take to work through the conflict. Resolution is intended to transform the parties in a lasting manner rather than to suppress the conflict, solve only an immediate problem, or accept a solution by fiat of a powerful individual (i.e., the library director).

Why wouldn't conflicting parties be willing to participate in seeking resolution?

If the parties were willing and able to confront the conflict, chances are they would have found a way to do so on their own. If one party believes it can "win" without compromising anything because it has more power, then it may see no reason to negotiate. If the parties believe that anything that could be "won" has already been "won," then they may have arrived at a stalemate. If being "right" is the ultimate win, then compromise might be viewed as an admission of having been "wrong." Each of these positions suggests a different stage of readiness to confront conflict constructively.

The stalemate situation is considered the "ripest" point for resolution because all other strategies for "winning" have been exhausted. Determining why the parties aren't willing to participate can be useful in facilitating a resolution.

The first step toward resolution is an agreement between/among the parties to confront the conflict, that is, to meet in an atmosphere of mutual respect and commitment to resolving the conflict through negotiation, even if it requires an extended period of time. The parties will have an opportunity to define their goals, identify perceived barriers to their goals, suggest possible compromises, and collaborate to resolve the conflict for the long term. The parties must agree not to walk away from the process or to impose or surrender to a one-sided resolution wherein one group gets everything it wants and the other group gets nothing. Depending on the severity of the conflict, a skilled third-party facilitator may be asked to oversee the process.

Additional strategies that may be applied in addition to negotiation and joint resolution meetings include these:

- Establishment of a superordinate goal, one that can be reached only when the conflicting groups work together and that focuses on combined group performance. This represents the library's overarching goal, but it gives the groups a shared goal, for example, constitute a task force to develop policy or constitute a committee representing all parties to solve problems related to or caused by the conflict.
- Change in the structural variables, such as reassigning staff members, combining conflicting departments, or separating conflicting departments by having them report to two persons who are not in conflict.
- Identify staff members from conflicting groups who are willing to negotiate and empower them to represent their group.
- Reduce competition for resources. If competition for resources underpins the conflict, then the parties must be convinced that the resolution will not change resource distribution. For this reason, resource decisions should be taken off the table when possible.

These situational controls can be seen as coercive, but they can be effective, especially when the groups themselves are allowed to recommend which measures should be applied, along with how and when they are applied. If the conflict is not defused, analyzed, confronted, and resolved at the library level, then other campus services may be enlisted to assist, such as an ombuds program, employee assistance program (counseling), HR mediation, legal counsel, and standing grievance policies.

INTERPERSONAL CONFLICT

Individuals as well as groups can conflict. An initial conflict between individuals will escalate quickly if it is fueled by threats, accusations, personal attacks, or bullying. Most adults have faced interpersonal conflict throughout their lives and have developed coping preferences or patterns of response to conflict. If conflict is perceived as a threat, a person is likely to exhibit the classic "fight or flight" response. Human beings are hardwired with a survival mechanism—the hormones adrenaline and cortisol—to prepare them for either reaction. When a threat is perceived, these hormones increase heart rate and respiration, shunt blood away from the stomach to muscles, and increase blood sugar. The "fight" response in adult coworkers can result in direct and unpleasant confrontation of the source of the threat and can even spill over into physical contact. The "flight" response has been socialized from literally running away from the threat to withdrawing from the threatening coworker, as if "playing dead" or exhibiting passive resistance (refusing to respond) or passive-aggressive behavior (responding indirectly). Passive-aggressive behavior can take the form of procrastination, stubbornness, sulking, feigning helplessness, or deliberate and repeated failure to accomplish a task. Both fight and flight are highly stressful, and neither response serves to resolve conflict.

So, how does one deal with interpersonal conflict with a coworker, especially if the conflict has become irrational or hostile? The answers sound simple, but they are very difficult to practice:

- Anticipate conflict, but don't go looking for it. Conflict is normal and experienced in almost every life situation. In and of itself, it is not shameful. How a person deals with it determines whether it will be a damaging experience or an opportunity for personal learning.
- Admit your role in the conflict. This is not about being right or wrong, or who started it, or whether or not you contributed to the conflict, but simply acknowledging that you are in conflict with

a coworker(s). Conflict arises from a perception of threat—that another stands in the way of reaching a goal—and the feelings provoked by threat are anxiety, fear, anger, and aggression.

- Revise your perception of threat. Does your coworker really have power over you—the potential to damage your work or your life—or is the threat to your work role or work identity? Is the threat catastrophic, merely uncomfortable, or perhaps more imagined than real? What is the real issue, and what is the goal you want to accomplish? What about the situation do you hope will change?
- Admit your dependence on the coworker(s). If you are not dependent in some way on the coworker to reach a goal, then there can be no conflict. If you and your coworker genuinely and respectfully agree to disagree on a matter of opinion, then you are not in conflict.
- Deescalate the intensity. If you are unable to resolve the fight or flight response, or if it is invoked repeatedly, the intensity of the conflict can compound and escalate beyond control. One party in the conflict may be able to check the intensity by making an offer of good faith, for example, acknowledging the other's position or needs as valid, offering to compromise, offering an apology, or making some attempt at reconciliation.

The inability to put any of these points into practice is by default, acceptance of the position of avoidance. Avoidance ignores one's own rights and perhaps the rights of others by trying to adapt, or making the best of a bad situation, or yielding to prevent further conflict. There are only two ways to resolve conflict—compromise or collaboration. Compromise can be negotiated, but it ensures that only some of each party's needs are met or are partially met. When conflicting parties have the ability to collaborate on a resolution, it is possible that the needs of both can be met fully.

A skilled supervisor can take responsibility for helping conflicted parties negotiate compromise and can encourage collaboration to resolve conflict. When this is not possible, the library's or the campus's HR staff may be able to assist. HR personnel have the advantage of impartiality and experience in resolving interpersonal conflicts and can offer a neutral meeting place to begin negotiation. The process involves facilitation meetings designed to help deescalate the intensity of the conflict, defuse perceived threats, guide communication so that each party might better understand the other's needs, and, eventually, explore the possibility of compromise. Several facilitation meetings might be required and may include drafting behavioral contracts for the conflicted parties to follow between meetings or further referral to employee assistance programs for individualized support. Many library managers think they should be able to solve any problem, see into the hearts of every employee, counsel them wisely, and successfully negotiate a resolution to every conflict. The truth is that people are complex and difficult to understand, and, in many situations, referring staff for help outside the library is the best response.

When conflict is beyond resolution or does not meet the definition of conflict (an expressed struggle between at least two parties who are interdependent and who believe one or more other parties are interfering with reaching a goal), then the situation may involve what is simply bad behavior—harassment or bullying. This is a very different matter and requires organizationwide action.

Are there any ways to prevent interpersonal conflict?

It is not likely that interpersonal conflict can be avoided altogether in life, but there are some things individuals can do to approach conflict constructively, especially if practiced at the onset of the identified "threat." The practices include recognizing and identifying one's immediate emotional response to a threat (anger, fear, pleasure, confusion, etc.), controlling the emotion (analyzing the emotion and waiting until it goes away before responding), recognizing others' emotions from their verbal and nonverbal messages, and stripping out the emotional content in order to respond to the problem rather than the threat. These approaches are suggested by theories of "emotional intelligence," which is not a native trait but can be learned as a skill set.

Coworker Harassment and Bullying

Harassment and bullying between coworkers can be looked at as specialized workplace hazards. Just like operating dangerous equipment or being exposed to toxic materials, these negative behaviors are harmful, even if the behavior occurs as a single, isolated incident. Harassment, including sexual harassment, has a legal definition and is "any physical or verbal conduct demonstrating hostility toward a person because of his or her age, sex, race, color, religion, national origin, disability or other legally protected status" (HRdirect, 2011). Harassment is against the law, and when it goes beyond a single incident and becomes so severe and pervasive that it permeates the work environment, it creates a "hostile work environment" or "hostile workplace."

Many colleges and universities have written antiharassment policies, provide antiharassment training for their employees, and protect claimants from retaliation. For example, Purdue University's (2011) Anti-Harassment Policy affirms that the institution "is committed to maintaining an environment that recognizes the inherent worth and dignity of every person; fosters tolerance, sensitivity, understanding and mutual respect; and encourages its members to strive to reach their potential. . . . Harassment in the workplace or the educational environment is unacceptable conduct and will not be tolerated." The policy extends beyond the workplace proper to include all university endeavors and relationships and even holds campus visitors and vendor representatives subject to the policy.

Harassment can take any form of expression—verbal, written, visual or graphic displays, gestures, or body language—and is intended to demean, ridicule, stereotype, insult, or threaten another person or persons who are members of a protected group. Harassment not directed at a person in a protected group and that otherwise breaks no federal law is generally referred to as "bullying." According to the Workplace Bullying Institute (2011), bullying is "repeated, health-harming mistreatment of one or more persons (the targets) by one or more perpetrators that takes one of more of the following forms: verbal abuse; offensive conduct/behaviors (including nonverbal) which are threatening, humiliating, or intimidating; work interference—sabotage—which prevents work from getting done." Sutton (2007: 49) provides a "dirty dozen" of bullying behaviors that includes "personal insults, invading a coworker's personal territory, uninvited physical contact, threats and intimidation, verbal and nonverbal; sarcastic jokes and teasing used as insult delivery systems, withering e-mails, status slaps intended to humiliate victims, public shaming or status degradation rituals, rude interruptions, two-faced attacks, dirty looks, and treating people as if they were invisible."

Bullies, or "jerks at work," include those who are abusive to a peer, but most bullies are bosses. Supervisors have legitimate authority, authorized by the organization, over their supervisees' work performance. Because of this power imbalance, supervisors are in a better position to bully those below them in the organization, even though logic might tell us they should be held to a higher standard. Because of the prevalence of bosses doing the bullying, bosses and their targets are discussed at length in the next chapter, while coworker bullies and their targets are discussed in this chapter. Bullying behavior is not restricted to those with reporting relationships—library users and coworkers in other campus units can be bullies, too.

According to Namie and Namie (2004), the leading researchers of workplace bullying, 28 percent of employees responding to a national survey reported having been bullied by a coworker (18 percent) or by a person below them in the organizational structure (10 percent). Having studied the phenomenon exclusively for more than ten years, the researchers identify three major types of workplace bullies (Namie and Namie, 2009). One is the personality bully, who knows no other way to operate in life. This "jerk at work" bullies anyone, anywhere, anytime in order to achieve a goal or meet a need. She or he is a jerk at home and in social situations, and the bad behavior extends to the workplace. There is little chance of personality bullies being rehabilitated. The second type is the opportunistic bully, for whom bullying has been an effective method to compete with others and to climb the organizational ladder. These bullies try to ingratiate themselves with those higher in the organizational structure, and they attack any peer or supervisee who is perceived as a competitor or a barrier to success. Their goal is strictly to gain a benefit at work, and outside work they are often regarded as generous and sensitive people. These bullies can stop, and the bad behavior can be arrested by disabling the system that has so reliably rewarded it. The third type of bully is the substance abuser, who tends toward explosive and unpredictable anger and paranoia or, depending on the substance, exhibits depression or lethargy. These bullies are not likely to stop until they are fired, hospitalized, or incarcerated.

Although it is difficult to say exactly how a bully selects a victim, Namie and Namie's research suggests that targets (their preferred term to "victim") do have some characteristics in common. Targets may refuse to acknowledge the bully's "superiority" in some way or resist subservience. They are oblivious to office politics and only want to be left alone to do their work. They are often the "go to" employee in a work group who is highly competent or technically proficient. They are generally well-liked and have good social skills. They are ethical and honest and may be more likely to be "whistle-blowers." The pattern appears to be that bullies, for whatever reason, target good employees rather than poor employees.

No type of bullying is permissible, and it is a management responsibility to create and enforce a zero-tolerance policy. If you are bullied by a coworker, a person you supervise, a library user, or another campus employee, and you are ready for it to stop, report it to your supervisor. Bullies are unlikely to stop unless management steps in to correct the behavior. If you stand by and watch a coworker being bullied and do nothing about it, you are enabling the bully and setting yourself or another coworker up to be the next target. The bully will pressure bystanders to take his or her side or to collaborate directly. If you have reported it and no action was taken, report it to your supervisor's supervisor and to campus HR personnel. Bullying is ethically and morally wrong and bad for the entire organization. It may take years to correct the hiring, retention, and disciplinary practices that support bullying and to eliminate bullies entirely, but it has to start somewhere, and that somewhere could be the library.

What and When to Tell a Supervisor

In addition to notifying a supervisor about episodes of bullying or harassment directed toward or witnessed by an employee, there are other important events that should be reported to a supervisor. Although situations vary greatly, some general occasions that require reporting include the following:

- Injuries sustained at work should be reported immediately so that first aid or a medical response can be initiated as soon as possible and, if necessary, reported for OSHA record-keeping requirements or workers' compensation claims. OSHA reporting is required for injuries or illnesses that cause loss of consciousness, result in sick days taken, require immediate medical treatment, or result in restricted work activities.
- Theft or "pilferage," which is taking small items on a regular basis, should be reported immediately. Uncomfortable as it may be to

bring this to a supervisor's attention, it is an obligation that falls under the employee's duty of loyalty. It is not necessary to accuse a specific person or group of employees unless there is absolute knowledge, but it is necessary to make the supervisor aware of any loss or losses. Any illegal or otherwise harmful activity in the workplace should be reported immediately—the presence or use of drugs or controlled substances, threats or acts of physical violence toward self or others, misuse of equipment or materials that could cause harm to another, and so forth.

- Not all personal medical conditions or health challenges that might affect performance or attendance must be reported, but disclosure is required if an employee intends to request a benefit such as FMLA leave or an ADA accommodation. For example, a pregnancy, injury, or illness that will require time away from work for treatment or an adjustment to regular duties must be disclosed as the basis for requesting extended or intermittent leave or a workplace accommodation. When possible, 30 days' notice should be provided when requesting these benefits.

- Disclosing other personal or medical conditions that do not rise to the level of requesting an accommodation or FMLA leave are up to the discretion of the employee. If disclosed, the supervisor may be able to help more quickly and effectively if one becomes ill while at work, whether from an illness or from the side effects of medication. Disclosure may prevent the supervisor from making assumptions about declines in motivation or ability and, if appropriate, enable the supervisor to refer the employee to an assistance program offered by the college or university. On the other hand, disclosure may create additional stress, and the employee may fear not being understood or accepted. If an employee decides to disclose an illness or condition requiring treatment, she or he should seek a private meeting with the supervisor and be prepared to describe what effect the illness or condition may have on work performance and attendance and, if known, the duration of treatment or time to recovery. It is not necessary to disclose the nature of the illness or medical condition, just the anticipated workplace effect and, when known, the duration.

- Before telling a supervisor about a coworker's aggravating or annoying behavior, (e.g., slacking off, passing work to others, taking credit for the work of others), it may be advisable to explain to the coworker, calmly and unemotionally, the impact this behavior is having on the work group and ask for the coworker's cooperation. If the behavior continues, then ask the supervisor for advice. If couched as a request for advice, the supervisor is notified effectively and can offer advice or intervene directly to remedy the situation.

- Resignations should be offered gracefully, in writing, and should include the date of the last expected working day. If the employer has stated an expected length of notice in an offer letter, an employment contract, or an employee manual that is considered part of the employment contract, then providing whatever constitutes "adequate" notice should be considered seriously. Assuming the employee wants to continue a good relationship with the institution and with coworkers, reasonable notice of resignation should be provided as a courtesy, if not an ethical duty.

Many personal situations are left to the discretion of the employee to report and can be difficult or painful to tell a supervisor. A basic rule of thumb is to disclose information when it affects one's ability to do the job or may endanger others. For example, if a person has obtained a restraining order against an abuser, then it would be helpful to disclose this information so that coworkers do not inadvertently tell the abuser the person's immediate location, what time the person gets off work, and so forth, and so that library security and campus police are better equipped to stop the abuser from breaking the order. If an employee has lost driving privileges from arrest or conviction as a result of DUI, for example, but is not expected to drive a library vehicle as a normal part of the job, then generally this would not require disclosure.

Summary

Libraries are organized into functional work groups wherein every staff member relies on others to accomplish work goals and advance the best interests of the library. Coworker relationships can promote the health and productivity of individuals but can also have negative effects during periods of interpersonal conflict. Although conflict is not always negative, it has the potential to disrupt the workplace if left unchecked. Support networks among coworkers can lend both social and instrumental assistance that promotes productivity and job satisfaction. Harassment and bullying are simply bad behavior that requires swift and emphatic organizational correction. The supervisor can play a key role in mitigating coworker conflict by influencing and motivating others and by solving small problems before they become big problems. The next chapter discusses the importance of the supervisor in increasing group performance, productivity, and job satisfaction.

REFERENCES

American Library Association. 2008. "Code of Ethics of the American Library Association." American Library Association. Amended January 22. www.ala.org/ala/issuesadvocacy/proethics/codeofethics/codeethics.cfm.

Chiaburu, Dan S., and David A. Harrison. 2008. "Do Peers Make the Place? Conceptual Synthesis and Meta-Analysis of Coworker Effects on Perceptions, Attitudes, OCBs, and Performance." *Journal of Applied Psychology* 93, no. 5: 1082–1103. doi:10.1037/0021-9010.93.5.1082.

Dittman, Melissa. 2003. "Study Links Co-Worker Support to Better Cardiovascular Health." *Monitor on Psychology* 34, no. 7: 11.

HRdirect. 2011. "The Harassment-Free Workplace." HRdirect. www.hrdirect.com/info/the-harassment-free-workplace/default.aspx.

"Human Relations School." 2001. In *World of Sociology*. Farmington, MI: Gale. www.credoreference.com/entry/worldsocs/human_relations_school.

Krackhardt, David. 1992. "The Strength of Strong Ties: The Importance of *Philos* in Organizations." In *Networks and Organizations: Structure, Form, and Action*, edited by Nitin Nohria and Robert G. Eccles, 216–239. Boston: Harvard Business School Press.

Mayo, Elton. 1945. *The Social Problems of an Industrial Civilization*. Boston: Division of Research, Graduate School of Business Administration, Harvard University.

Montgomery, Jack G., and Eleanor I. Cook. 2005. *Conflict Management for Libraries: Strategies for a Positive, Productive Workplace*. Chicago: American Library Association.

Namie, Gary, and Ruth Namie. 2004. "Workplace Bullying: How to Address America's Silent Epidemic." *Employee Rights and Employment Policy Journal* 8, no. 2: 315–333.

———. 2009. *The Bully at Work: What You Can Do to Stop the Hurt and Reclaim Your Dignity on the Job*. 2nd ed. Naperville, IL: Sourcebooks. Kindle Edition.

Northern Illinois University. 2011. "Statement on Professional Behavior of Employees: University Collegiality Policy." Northern Illinois University.

Approved by University Council, May 6, 1998; Update Approved January 26, 2011; Last updated February 1. www.niu.edu/provost/policies/appm/II21.shtml.

Purdue University. 2011. "University Policies, Ethics: Anti-Harassment Compliance." Purdue University. Last revised May 1. www.purdue.edu/policies/pages/ethics/x_2_1.shtml.

Rath, Tom. 2006. *Vital Friends: The People You Can't Afford to Live Without.* Washington, DC: Gallup Press.

Sutton, Robert. 2007. "By Invitation: Building the Civilized Workplace." *McKinsey Quarterly* 2007, no. 2: 47–55. www.washburn.edu/faculty/rweigand/McKinsey/McKinsey-Building-The-Civilized-Workplace.pdf.

Wilmot, William W., and Joyce L. Hocker. 2007. *Interpersonal Conflict.* 7th ed. Boston: McGraw-Hill.

Workplace Bullying Institute. 2011. "Definition of Workplace Bullying." Workplace Bullying Institute. www.workplacebullying.org/targets/problem/definition.html.

supervising others

There is a human resource saying: **"The boss *is* the job."** The adage means the supervisor is the make-it-or-break-it factor in employees' job success and satisfaction. Even the most skilled and hard-working supervisor cannot turn a terrible job into a wonderful job or make someone love work he or she does not find challenging and rewarding, but every supervisor has the power to motivate, coach, mentor, and develop those who report to him or her. Conversely, poor supervision contributes to poor performance, low productivity, high turnover, and eventually to a person's loss of faith in the purpose and value of his or her work. Some version of "I hate my boss" is frequently given as a primary reason for leaving a job. Whether serving as the supervisor or the supervisee, familiarity with the responsibilities and expectations of the supervisory role can encourage mutual understanding between both, and it may even improve job performance.

Foundation and Philosophy

Supervision is a management function wherein a single person has day-to-day oversight of the work and welfare of one or more employees. Supervisors are usually involved in the selection and hiring processes, in orienting and training new employees, and in evaluating and, when necessary, disciplining employees. Historically, supervision has had a bad reputation. Around 1910, Frederick Taylor established a school of thought called "scientific management." Taylor was a mechanical engineer who studied efficiency in industrial work settings. He was the first person to espouse scientific observation of work tasks to produce a desired result—getting more production with less effort by finding the single best way to perform a task. The supervisor's job was to select, train, and develop employees and to enforce this "single best way." Unfortunately, Taylor believed that workers themselves were not smart enough to control or improve work processes and that oversight by a manager or supervisor was required. Taylor was the first to suggest that work processes could be improved by applying scientific methodology, such as observation and measurement, and was the first to suggest that the supervisor's job was to instruct and train employees. Although Taylor's (1911) principles may be considered elitist and outdated today, they provided early recognition of the importance of supervision and the supervisor's role in promoting the practices of quality control and quality improvement.

Supervision

In libraries and many other types of organizations, supervisors are often selected or promoted based on their previous job performance. The assumption is that once someone has proven the ability to do a task or manage a process and is highly motivated, he or she will be able to manage the task or process when others do it and receives higher pay in exchange for being held accountable for the work of others. Supervision is only one function of the larger role of manager, and it requires an entirely different skill set than librarianship. The supervisor is responsible for the performance and productivity of each individual and that of the collective work group. Supervisors are often "middle" managers, sandwiched in between higher leaders, who have a mission, goals, and objectives for the library; and their supervisees, who have individual goals and objectives for their work and work lives. The middle manager–supervisor stands as a proxy for the library's higher leaders and is expected to translate the library's goals and objectives into actions that result in the library achieving its mission. If there is a disconnect between leadership and the proxy supervisor, the supervisor is expected to identify and repair the slippage.

Academic libraries spend about 50 percent of their total budgets on salaries and wages (National Center for Education Statistics, 2011), and most managers will say that at least 50 percent of their time is spent managing people as opposed to managing processes or resources. Both in money and time, considerable resources are spent on library personnel. Despite this, supervision of a work group or department is often added to the top of an existing set of position duties as if it were just one more routine task to be done rather than the priority of the position. It takes effort, attention, and time to become a good supervisor—all with little or no training. Library education programs rarely teach supervisory skills, and universities rarely work at developing supervision below the highest leadership levels. The new supervisor might be offered a one- or two-day workshop by the campus HR unit, but it is likely to concentrate on compliance with internal policies. Most of what an individual knows about effective or ineffective supervision comes from his or her previous experience as a supervisee. Former supervisors have modeled desirable and undesirable behaviors, and most people can easily identify the good and bad supervisors they have had in their careers and describe in detail specific characteristics of both.

The best way to become an excellent supervisor is by making a prolonged and conscious effort to improve basic skills. The basic supervisory skill set includes expert knowledge of a library process, function, or service and the abilities to communicate effectively, to solve problems, and to motivate and coach staff members.

EXPERT KNOWLEDGE

Some combination of expert knowledge, skills, and abilities will be required qualifications for any supervisory position. The organization in general, and those supervised by the position, will expect the supervisor to know more about a library process, function, or service than anyone else and to maintain this lead in order to inform, train, retrain, and evaluate the work of participating individuals. Fulfilling this basic expectation of supervisors requires continuing education, study, and professional development to stay ahead of the curve, especially as academic libraries and higher education in general undergo fundamental changes in the way they do business. An individual supervisor's interests in a field or subfield can change over time or can shift to focus on something entirely outside the unit's responsibility. If a supervisor has lost all interest in the substance, content, and purpose of the unit's work and has lost his or her own motivation for further mastery and improvement, it becomes difficult to motivate the performance of others. The best supervisors are passionate about their area of expertise. Disinterest is hard to hide and can be infectious. When this happens, the best solution might be to "follow the heart" and look for a position in the new area of interest. If the supervisor is not rewarded by his or her work, it is unlikely that the supervisees will be either. Expert knowledge may be a predicate for quality supervision, but it is certainly not the only or even the most important factor in successful supervision.

INTERPERSONAL COMMUNICATION

Supervisors spend most of their day communicating—face-to-face with individuals and groups, reading and writing e-mails, or on the phone. We've been communicating all our lives, and it seems like we should be very good at it by the time we reach adulthood, but it is probably the single most difficult supervisory skill to master and then practice consistently. Supervisors need to be good communicators, because their staffs rely on them to convey important information and instructions about work and to relay messages to and from external sources. Communication research suggests that a message must be sent an average of four times before it is understood by the receiver. Communicating effectively takes effort and time—resources that are in short supply and high demand. The greater the rate of organizational change, the greater the effort and time it takes for a supervisor to communicate with those who report directly to him or her. This helps to explain why it is so difficult to improve communication skills and why it takes so long to achieve a high level of mastery.

In the workplace, all communication takes place within the context of relationships; that is, messages are interpreted based on what is known about the speaker (or writer)—past experiences, level of trust, and estimations of the speaker's credibility. These factors not only inform our response to messages but also influence our perception of the relationship, both positively and negatively. If the supervisor has established good relationships with supervisees already, then effective communication is much easier because the internal "noise" level (thoughts or feelings that interfere with the message) is reduced. The greatest relationship "cement" is the frequency, quality, consistency, and meaningfulness of interpersonal conversations.

Increasing the frequency of interpersonal conversations with supervisees is relatively easy when all are collocated but requires a conscious effort to sit down periodically with each person to share feedback on the substance or quality of his or her work or to ask questions about his or her work needs. Simply going beyond greeting a person in the morning, saying good night in the evening, and having routine staff meetings indicates the supervisor's interest, attention, and availability to each individual supervisee. These interactions can be "tucked in" to the workday without interrupting either the supervisor's or supervisee's work if the supervisor looks for the opportunity to do so.

The quality of interpersonal communications relies in part on the scope, depth, and differentiation of message content. Talking about and listening to what supervisees have to say about all aspects of work, rather than repeating the same conversation over and over, gives the general message that all work topics are on the table; there are no "sacred cows." It also helps correct the tendency to address only the most comfortable topics and ignore the uncomfortable ones. Striking a balance among topics of conversation to address the supervisor's needs, the employee's needs, and the library's needs lends organizational perspective to the substance of communications.

The clarity and consistency of the supervisor's messages to supervisees are interrelated aspects of communication. If a message is unclear, the person receiving the message isn't able to gauge its consistency with previous messages. If a message is clear but inconsistent with previous messages, the receiver might doubt its credibility or importance. Clarity can be enhanced if a long and complex message is sequenced into shorter, direct sentences and alternated with periodic requests for acknowledgment or questions. Such requests should not be intimidating ("Is that clear to you?" or "Do you understand?") but genuine and open-ended questions ("Does that make sense?" or "Would that be something you'd agree with, or do you have other ideas about it?"). When delivering an uncomfortable message, one can improve clarity by avoiding transitional qualifiers such as "but," "however," and "although." They tend to minimize or negate the first part of the message and connect it to, rather than differentiate it from, the second part of the message, for example: "You have always been helpful to patrons, but you make a lot of mistakes." Eliminating the qualifier and separating the two ideas in time acknowledges what the person has done well in the past and sets a goal for the future, for example: "You have always been helpful to patrons and that is very important. Now, we can move on to developing another important aspect of your performance, which is accuracy."

Meaningfulness of communications is related to the perceived importance of conversational content, the depth of the discussion, and the amount of information exchanged. If the exchange is too brief or interrupted more than is absolutely necessary or if the supervisor is distracted, then the impression is that the message is not very important. If the exchange is long and rambling, the message gets lost, which signals that whatever the message was, it must not have been very important. If the conversation is all speaking and no listening, no information is exchanged, and the message tends to go in one ear and out the other. This is especially true when the message consists entirely of complaints, when one person does all the talking while the other does all the listening.

PROBLEM SOLVING

Problem solving is a cognitive process through which people identify undesirable situations or conditions and then postulate explanations, answers, or actions that will resolve the undesirable situation or condition. For library supervisors, familiar problems have to do with spreading scarce resources, gaining new resources, distributing work so that it is equitable yet efficient, and meeting competing or conflicting demands. Regardless of the nature of the challenge, supervisees look to the supervisor first to solve generic problems in the workplace and then problems reported by individual staff members. The best supervisors are responsive to problems and skilled at resolving them. This does not necessarily mean having a quick and straight-line solution to every problem but drawing on both their expert knowledge of a process or function and their good communication skills to further define the problem and to launch the process of problem solving. There are a number of problem-solving approaches described in the business literature (PDCA or the Deming Cycle, the Simplex Process, the Straw Man approach, etc.), but most follow a series of steps resembling the research process or scientific method. The first step is identifying and describing the problem. What seems an obvious and urgent problem to one person might be perceived as only a small aggravation by another. Without making assumptions about the cause or source of the problem, it is useful to gather as much information as possible from affected staff and colleagues to evaluate the nature, frequency, and urgency of the problem. Once the problem is described and verified, the requirements for a solution should be determined, for example, must not cost money, must not create additional or side effect problems or shift the problem to another department, must resolve the problem for the long term, must be aligned with organizational goals, and so forth. Once the problem has been described and the requirements for a solution have been specified, then potential solutions can be explored and the most feasible or satisfactory solution chosen. Those directly affected by the problem should always be involved in offering potential solutions and evaluating and selecting the most feasible solution. Just as the research process does not end with identifying a single and final answer, problem solving does not end with identifying a solution. The solution must be implemented and tested and, if not satisfactory, refined further or taken all the way back to the drawing board.

MOTIVATING AND COACHING OTHERS

An employee's potential to perform at peak levels is based on two major factors: motivation and ability; having one without the other results in reduced job performance. Academic libraries often do a good job screening and hiring based on applicants' demonstrated and potential abilities and a good job of maintaining and improving their employees' knowledge, skills, and abilities after hire. Unlike ability, motivation is more difficult to specify and manipulate because it is largely intrinsic and driven by a person's readiness to act in order to reach an internal set of goals or objectives. Once a person is motivated, he or she has the potential to profit from coaching. "Coach," in the sense of trainer or teacher, was a nineteenth-century slang application of the word to a university student's tutor—the conveyance that carried the student from one level to the next, just as a horse-drawn coach carried travelers from place to place.

Motivation

There are a number of approaches to motivation, but, historically, research on motivation has produced models with unusually high levels of agreement. That is, there are relatively few conflicting theories of motivation, and some of the most widely accepted indicators of high job engagement have measurable neurobiological effects. In academic libraries, more of the work has become intellectual (involving cognition, understanding, problem solving, and decision making), and less of the work is now routine and repetitive (involving labeling, stamping, shelving, and filing). Consequently, external motivators such as pay, competition, disciplinary action, and numeric scores on performance evaluations are not highly effective motivators per se. It is difficult to scare or threaten someone into better performance of intellectual work or to pay someone enough money to effectively coerce creativity or innovation.

David Rock, an authority on coaching, views motivation as the key driver in increasing employee engagement. Similar to student engagement, employee engagement is the level of involvement, commitment, and attachment to the organization, its mission, and library coworkers. Engagement influences an employee to devote greater discretionary effort to his or her work. Discretionary effort is the difference between the effort required just to get by at work and the effort to go above and beyond the minimum requirements. Because employees make their own decisions about discretionary effort, engagement is a gift offered voluntarily by employees and, by definition, cannot be coerced or demanded. Rock (2008) further believes that the basis of employee engagement lies in a single organizing principle of the brain, which is to minimize danger and maximize reward. Physical and emotional responses to dangerous or threatening situations have been studied since the late 1920s, for example, the "fight or flight" response (Cannon, 1927), but responses to reward situations have been studied only since the 1970s, for example, the "flow" theory (Csikszentmihalyi, 1975). Rock describes five "domains" of motivators/rewards that increase employee engagement. They are literally internal or "intrinsic" motivators; that is, they can be measured by distinct neurobiological responses of an individual (blood pressure, skin conductance, brain activity, levels of certain hormones). Rock (2008) devised the "SCARF" model, which represents five domains of threat/reward: status, certainty, autonomy, relatedness, and fairness:

1. **Status** is a person's valuation of himself or herself in relation to others in a group, for example, within the immediate work group, the peer group, or the entire organization. Status is about the individual's perceived relative importance to the group or, in animal terms, rank in the "pecking order." The importance of status rewards and of status as a motivator of engagement varies greatly among individuals. For some, a status reward might be mastering a skill, which allows comparisons of the "before" self to the "after" self. For others, it is being acknowledged as the most skilled member of a group at one particular thing or another. Familiar workplace status rewards are praise or recognition, awards, and job promotions. For some, title changes that make a job sound more significant or powerful are valuable status rewards, as are business cards that reflect the preferred title. For others, getting the "corner office" or a similar desirable work space might be considered a status reward. A certain amount of direct competition with others, especially if it is entered into voluntarily and perceived as fair, for example, selecting one job candidate over many others, may be perceived as an opportunity for a status reward. However, when the threat potential is high, for example, cutting similar positions based on the relative merit of the incumbents, competition to survive can lead to unethical behaviors, such as cheating and sabotage.

2. **Certainty** is the degree to which we are able to predict conditions or events. We like knowing where we are going—literally and figuratively. If a supervisor's or the library's expectations are not clear, our brains have to work harder trying to predict the desired behaviors or actions—shuffling through variant responses and strategizing a response that is likely to cover all the bases—and this is a needless and draining distraction from reaching the real objective, meeting the supervisor's expectations. At present,

academic environments are characterized by unprecedented levels of uncertainty, and, to one degree or another, this may remain the norm for the foreseeable future. Uncertainty is a threat condition and can result in disengagement. Even though no supervisor can control destiny, every supervisor can take action to decrease the level of uncertainty, and this begins on a personal level. If a supervisor is unpredictable, behaves inconsistently, changes priorities too often, or hoards information, this compounds any threat generated by organizational uncertainty. Even small actions can increase certainty and reduce the level of threat, for example, scheduling regular meetings and sticking to the schedule, breaking down large strategic plans into a series of smaller specific steps, providing reasonable completion deadlines and benchmarks for quality, and repeating statements or instructions multiple times. Small certainties are rewards and motivators for many employees, because they increase the employee's probability of success.

3. **Autonomy** is the real or perceived level of personal control an employee has in the work environment and over the conditions of work; that is, how much an individual is permitted to decide about his or her work. Working in a team tends to decrease autonomy but has potential rewards in other domains, such as status and relatedness. Allowing control (individual decisions) with certainty (agreed upon policies or practices) over work is a reward. Flex time and compressed workweeks are autonomy rewards, as are making personal choices about organizing and decorating work spaces, making point-of-need decisions without having to consult a supervisor, and selecting professional development activities rather than having them prescribed. To those who find autonomy highly rewarding, micromanagement is the ultimate threat to engagement.

4. **Relatedness** is a person's perception of belonging to or affiliation with a group. The group can be departmental coworkers, a professional association, a work team, a committee, or an entire library staff. The practice of banding together is deeply human,

and the ability to quickly recognize another as "friend" (likely to reward) or "foe" (likely to threaten) is thought to be a survival mechanism that evolved prior to the development of civilization. Sports teams, law enforcement officers, and military personnel wear uniforms in order to recognize "friends" quickly. Wearing a replica team shirt or clothing with a university logo is one way individuals demonstrate a strong sense of relatedness or group affiliation. Personal and organizational rewards of relatedness are discussed at greater length in Chapter 3 under "Coworker Support and Cohesion." The supervisor of a group for whom relatedness is rewarding can encourage safe connections, not just within the group, but within the library and the entire institution by offering rewards such as appointment to committees, arranging job rotations in other units, encouraging mentor–protégé pairings, and planning office celebrations and group recognition events.

5. **Fairness** is the perception that employment transactions are equitable and consistent and follow established policies and practices. Fairness can be a reward in and of itself, and unfairness can carry strong threat potential. In most aspects of life, we expect justice to mean that goodness is rewarded and evil is punished, and the perception of fairness is as important as fairness in fact. For example, discrepancies in pay that are misunderstood, or for which no rationale has been offered, are perceived as unfairness, even by persons who believe they are fairly compensated themselves. Assigning more of the same work to an employee who is highly competent and less of the same work to a moderately competent employee is perceived as an unfair practice even though it may be more efficient and more satisfactory to both employees. Assigning a less desirable task to the same person all the time because the person does it cheerfully may be perceived as unfair. The threat potential of perceived unfairness can be reduced by providing as much transparency as possible— sharing as much information about the action as possible (what, when, how, why, and who), providing detailed and truthful rationales for the action, offering repeated and consistent commu-

nications of the information, and letting staff determine to the extent possible their own rules or procedure for how the action will be implemented locally.

One of the most difficult conflicts for a supervisor is to take an action that might seem unfair but that maintains the confidentiality of personal information. This can arise when the supervisor understands the reason for an action in detail but is not at liberty to share it entirely with others, for example, an employee is permitted to work at home for an extended period of time after his or her unsuccessful suicide attempt (or similar sensitive and intensely personal situations) or knows why a person has not been reappointed but does not share the reasons or offer an opinion about it with the rest of the work group. In these cases, the supervisor is advised not to share knowledge of the events leading up to the action but simply the fact of the action.

The five domains of the SCARF model serve as a broad template for understanding rewards and motivators and their potential for the opposite—to threaten and deter or demotivate people. Individuals attach different levels of importance to status, certainty, autonomy, relatedness, and fairness, and a work group or team may include those motivated by a mixture of rewards, or their importance can vary with environmental conditions, for example, given the current economic challenges facing higher education, certainty may be considered a premium reward by many employees.

Coaching

The derivation of the word "coach" refers to conveying a person from one location to the next or from a lower level to a higher level, and supervisory coaching is one aspect of transformational leadership. In transformational leadership, the supervisor/leader helps the supervisee/follower to change in some permanent and fundamental way and presumably in a way that develops the supervisee's job performance. The practice of coaching for improved work performance became widespread during the 1980s, and over 800 hardcover books on the topic are available. There are numerous coaching models, including GROW, STEPPA, and SUCCESS, which are acronyms for dimensions or steps of the coaching process; for example, Goals, Reality, Obstacles/Options, and Way forward are steps of the GROW model.

Coaching is performance related, follows a specific agenda and goals, and is a short-term proposition. Coaching is different from mentoring and counseling and may be best understood in academe as closely related to Socratic teaching—or asking a set of guided questions. Coaching is about posing the important questions: What are your job or performance goals? What are you doing now that stands in the way of reaching your goals? What do you need to do differently in the future to reach your goals? What training or development activities would help you? Coaching can be applied to a number of domains in the library workplace, including knowledge coaching (to learn new content), skills coaching (to develop technical or communication skills), results coaching (to focus on productivity), and development coaching (to prepare for new or potential roles in the library).

The greatest return on the coaching investment is from those who are motivated to reach their peak performance and develop to their highest potential. Conventional business wisdom dictates that coaching is not for those with performance problems or those who have low potential to make future contributions to the organization. Many businesses would consider this investment a waste. However, in academic library settings, coaching is often considered a useful method to address and remediate poor performance, and, in fairness to the employee, it should be used before the formal disciplinary process is invoked. Coaching is also useful to help a new employee get "up to speed" during the probationary or initial employment period.

Coaching takes time, effort, and personal attention on the part of the supervisor and the supervisee. On the part of the supervisee, it also requires a willingness to consider feedback impersonally, to reflect on past performance, and to set goals for the future. If coaching is intended to remediate poor performance, then it should be initiated as soon as performance falters. If the supervisor and the supervisee have tried numerous times to address problems without success, or mutual resentment or lack of trust has come between them, they may have lost the neutrality required for effective coaching. Coaching for improved work performance generally involves a series of four steps:

1. **Develop trust.** This begins with the offer to coach a supervisee and involves explaining the process and setting any ground rules. Ground rules could include agreements to stay solution focused rather than problem focused, to refrain from blaming others or the library, and to be truthful and honest.

2. **Set goals.** The supervisee begins to set personal goals for work. Some goals may be longer term (become a better communicator, expand the role of the job or the position, manage a large project), while others may be shorter term objectives (report to work every day for a month, improve speed with which a certain task is done without losing accuracy or quality, answer e-mail messages the same day). During this process, it is not helpful to question why the supervisee thinks the goal or objective is worthy, only to guide the supervisee in identifying goals or objectives. The initial list of goals should be short, precise, and directional. The purpose here is to encourage the supervisee to set his or her own goals so that he or she can assume control of self-management. Some theorists, the best known being Marcus Buckingham and Donald Clifton (2001), believe it is a waste of time to set goals designed to address a supervisee's perceived weakness. Buckingham and Clifton believe, based on research, that setting goals based on a person's strengths is far more productive. They define a "strength" as any activity that makes you feel effective and successful, that you actively look forward to doing, that makes you feel inquisitive and focused when you are doing it, and that makes you feel fulfilled and authentic after you've done it. They suggest that 75–80 percent of coaching should be aimed toward developing strengths and 20–25 percent aimed at minimizing or neutralizing weaknesses.

3. **Offer support.** Once the coach has assisted the supervisee to set goals, to discover and avoid barriers to goal achievement, and to identify actions or efforts the supervisee thinks he or she needs to adopt to meet goals, then the work has to happen—carrying through with the actions necessary for change. The coach's role during this period is to offer encouragement, impart a sense of

confidence, and celebrate small victories. This can be done in small, short bursts across a period of time, for example, stopping by to check in two or three times a week or in one or more 30-minute meetings.

4. **Provide wrap-up/follow-up.** The coach's role is to assist the supervisee in evaluating his or her progress, to ask for measurements or evidence of the results, and to ask for suggestions on improving the coaching process. Direct praise and positive feedback should be offered to the supervisee for making an attempt to change his or her behavior and for successful goal achievement.

Toxic Bosses

The principle "The boss *is* the job" may be felt most deeply when the supervisor is toxic—a screamer, a hypercritical micromanager, and/or an emotionally volatile and vindictive person. Such bosses have been described as "bullies," and bully bosses can target a single employee or an entire group. According to Namie and Namie (2004: 325–327), 71 percent of bullies are bosses; the remaining bully their peers, and a few even bully their supervisors. Women are slightly more likely than men to be bullies and are far more likely to be the target of a bully. As in domestic abuse situations, workplace bullying is enabled by fear, shame, and silence. Targets who do complain may be criticized as "too sensitive," having misunderstood the bully's intentions or meaning, told to "work it out" with the bully, or even be accused of having provoked the bully somehow. Although it's hard to say with any certainty what causes supervisors to become bullies, there are theories. One common characteristic of adult bullies is that they are controlling in order to compete or to satisfy personal gains by exploiting others. One theory offers that bullies use power to hide their fear of incompetence and believe their power, credibility, or status is under constant attack within the larger organization. They cut others down to aggrandize themselves. Another theory suggests that bullies are simply opportunists who have learned that "tough bosses" are the ones who are promoted. This may be true in highly competitive business environments where the culture emphasizes winning at any cost, and it is thought to be one reason the United States has been slow to address workplace bullying, but how does this relate to academic libraries? In higher education, where the typical policy is to share governance, individual library work groups have little or no real power to control a college or university, monetary rewards are relatively small, and recognition by promotion in rank or pay grade can take years to earn. In the absence of business rewards such as corporate power, money, and promotion, status among one's peers becomes an overworked means of recognition and reward in colleges and universities. This can lead to perceived status differences based on relatively small and sometimes irrelevant measures. Seniority often becomes a basis for "pecking order." Placement on the progress-toward-tenure or continuous appointment schedule, the award of tenure and rank, the perceived trendiness of skills or knowledge possessed, the number and type of publications, and assignment to special projects can all enhance a person's self-esteem and status among the peer group. These external status rewards can be very powerful and bring out the competitive bully just as quickly as huge pay increases, stock options, and private jets bring them out in corporate life. Unfortunately, academic libraries are not rarefied organizations immune to the problem, as evidenced in this anonymous blog posting:

> [My supervisor] is a monster. She singles out employees for no apparent reason and then makes their lives hell. She specializes in public humiliation and intimidation. In the last four years, she has driven 15 people out of the reference department, a department that has 10 people at full strength. Some of these people left the profession entirely. The administration knows about her behavior, but they protect her since they have all been working together for 20 years. (Anonymous, 2010)

Preventing both harassment and bullying is an institutional and library leadership responsibility. There are clear and direct policies to prevent and intervene in cases of harassment, which violates federal and related state laws protecting groups that historically have been denied civil rights. Unfortunately, there are not equally clear and direct policies to prevent and intervene in cases of bullying. It would be useful if colleges and universities developed policies that would define bullying, clearly described it as unacceptable in any form, and extended the legal protection against a hostile workplace to everyone. Such policies could create enforcement processes, provide staff training to identify and report this generic form of harassment, incorporate it into performance evaluations, and provide some means to rehabilitate or remove the offender. Collegiality statements may describe the expected behavior and attitude toward coworkers but generally skirt the bullying issue altogether by lacking the details of reporting and intervention processes.

Performance Evaluation

Performance evaluation or "performance appraisal" season is rarely anticipated with pleasure, and both supervisors and supervisees often dread the process. Many supervisors want to get performance evaluations done and signed as quickly as possible so that they can move on to other tasks. Performance evaluation has become routine, there are few consequences tied to evaluation results, their annual recurrence is too distant in time from specific positive or negative behaviors to be meaningful, and the process tends to reward "poor" employees with more of the supervisor's time and attention than it rewards "good" employees.

Nevertheless, libraries practice performance evaluation using a process developed by the institution and is usually based on elements of the employee's position description or a position "questionnaire." A position questionnaire is a form that asks set questions about the responsibilities and compensable factors of a position and is developed when a new position is requested and authorized. Employees subject to the Fair Labor Standards Act (FLSA), sometimes called "hourly" employees and including those who are members of a labor organization, will have well-specified evaluation forms. Some evaluation forms include an additional set of core characteristics, organizational values, or expectations of all employees. Most ask the supervisor to rate the employee across the criteria using descriptors that translate to a numeric score, for example "outstanding = 5," "satisfactory = 3," "needs improvement = 1." Table 4.1 illustrates a "menu" of criteria often found in performance evaluation forms for classified staff members. Combinations of criteria, rating scales, and opportunities to provide narrative comments can vary widely depending on the method adopted by an institution and may mix weighted or unweighted checklists with supervisor and staff narratives.

Table 4.1

PERFORMANCE EVALUATION "MENU" FOR CLASSIFIED STAFF

SECTION OF FORM	HOW COMPLETED
Job Responsibilities	
A brief listing of major job duties that can be weighted by percentage of time spent or ranked in importance	Staff member completes this section using existing position description and performance management standards, if available. Supervisor assigns a rating label, for example, Outstanding, Satisfactory, Needs Improvement, Unsatisfactory. The rating label may or may not equate to a metric—4 points, 3 points, 2 points, and so forth. The supervisor may have the opportunity to comment on the staff member's performance of each responsibility or to make to comments on overall performance. If job responsibilities will change for the next evaluation cycle, the position description will be updated to reflect the change(s).
Goal Attainment	
Goal attainment during the current cycle	Supervisor assigns a rating label for each goal set during the evaluation meeting from the previous cycle and may have the opportunity to comment.
Goals set for the next cycle	Staff member and supervisor set goals for the next evaluation cycle.
Development Plan	Staff member and supervisor identify training, coaching, or mentoring activities for the next cycle.
Performance Factors/ Dimensions	
Flexibility Initiative/innovation Teamwork/collaboration Quality of work Productivity Decision making Dependability Attendance/punctuality Communication	Supervisor assigns a rating label to each factor/dimension and may have the opportunity to comment. The factors/ dimensions might be a standardized set for all staff, or the supervisor might select the most relevant factors/ dimensions from a larger list provided by the institution. The listing provides examples of typical performance factors/dimensions.

Required Competencies	
Knowledge Skills Abilities	Taken from the KSAs enumerated in the position classification and position description, the supervisor assigns a rating label to each basic competency required for successful performance and may have the opportunity to comment. These ratings can also be taken into consideration for planning staff development during the next cycle.
Core Values	
Commitment to diversity Commitment to community Commitment to service	Some institutions include core value statements in evaluation forms, and the listing provides examples. Supervisor assigns a rating label to each core value based on the staff member's demonstration by action or behavior and may have the opportunity to comment.
Overall Assessment	Supervisor assigns a rating label that most closely describes the staff member's overall job performance or sums the previously assigned metric scores and equates the total to a rating label. Most often, the supervisor has the opportunity to offer comments in this section.
Supervision	
Leadership Performance management Staff welfare	If the staff member supervises others, a section like this may be included prior to the *Overall Assessment* section. Supervisor assigns a rating to each supervisory function and may have the opportunity to comment. The listing provides examples of typical supervisory functions. In some cases, staff may be asked to contribute to their supervisor's evaluation.

Faculty or professional librarians and professional staff members will have different evaluation forms and separate processes, and the forms are likely to be broader in scope and generally ask for more narrative evaluation than checklist items. The evaluation process for exempt or professional employees occurs annually and involves a direct supervisor's evaluation, but it can also include an administrative evaluation, peer evaluations, and supervisees' evaluations. When all three are used together, the practice is called "360 degree evaluation." In general, library professional staff members are evaluated along many of the same criteria as classified staff members, but other criteria reflecting librarywide responsibilities are added, for example, budget and finance, facilities management, information systems, HR, marketing, donor relations, and so forth. In addition to evaluating the performance of specific duties and responsibilities assigned to professional employees, additional criteria can include "organizational impact" or the effectiveness of decisions and activities designed to produce broad desired outcomes, planning and organizing, implementing university policies and supporting university goals, managing special projects, and establishing and maintaining relationships with other campus units. Because the person's job performance is expected to advance the library's core mission, and the position may be unique within the library, long written passages are usually required to explain the context, impact, goal attainment, and achievements of the person. Although the evaluation forms may be as highly structured as classified staff evaluation forms and may use the same or similar rating labels as classified staff evaluation forms, professional staff evaluation forms rely more on employee-provided information, for example, an annual report or collected evidence, and the supervisor's assessment of the quantity, quality, and effectiveness of performance in terms of the person's overall contributions to the library's success. Performance evaluations for faculty librarians or librarians with continuous appointment are discussed at length in Chapter 6.

The evaluation process does serve some important purposes in colleges and universities. It establishes a fair, institutionwide process that measures performance using the same "ruler" for all employees within the same status category. It can establish the minimum eligibility requirement for merit increases when money is available (e.g., employees who receive ratings of satisfactory or higher). It can be used by the supervisor as a mechanism to give fair warning to employees who may face disciplinary action if performance continues to be unsatisfactory. Completed performance evaluations can and should be used by the campuswide HR unit or other administrators to identify gross supervisor error, such as abusive or demeaning language or statements, threats, or inappropriate comments related to a person's membership in a protected status group. Results can be used to assess performance evaluation across an entire classification of employees, for example, how did supervisors rate the performance of employees in similar or same jobs this year? This can help identify recurring problems and training needs at the institutional level.

The annual performance evaluation is not the best way to provide corrective feedback, as it is a summative evaluation, that is, a cumulative assessment of how well the supervisee has met performance require-ments or achieved a set of goals during an entire year. It provides a long-term record for the institution of a supervisee's performance, and it ver-ifies that the supervisor has met the obligation to evaluate supervisees. Throughout the year leading up to this summative evaluation, the super-visor has numerous opportunities to provide formative evaluation, that is, more frequent diagnostic evaluations to identify supervisory expec-tations in need of clarification by the supervisee, training that might improve performance, or a supervisee's need for additional demonstra-tion, teaching, or role modeling by the supervisor. Formative evaluation also lets supervisees know immediately when they have done something well and permits correcting any errors or misjudgments as they occur. The coaching process can be used during the year to bring a supervisee's performance up to minimum standard in advance of the annual evalua-tion, or it can be initiated as the result of a poor evaluation.

Performance evaluation should not be approached as a pro forma or perfunctory activity. It is an opportunity for the supervisor to express appreciation for what supervisees have done well and to thank them for their continued efforts. It is also an opportunity to provide constructive feedback or offer coaching for those who are not meeting expectations. It should document job performance as specifically and as accurately as possible, especially if performance, work habits, or attendance do not meet minimum expectations. Encouraging the illusion of adequate or above average performance when a supervisee does not perform at high levels is not a favor. It prevents the supervisee from improving his or her performance and discredits the basis for future disciplinary action the supervisor may wish to initiate.

Progressive Discipline

Not every supervisee performs at high levels or can be coached to improve the level of his or her performance. This happens more often than anyone would like, but it is a reality of supervision. Recognizing this as a fact of life, colleges and universities have established measures for progressive discipline. "Progressive" discipline refers to a series of actions that esca-late the consequences of continued unsatisfactory performance. Because employee discipline procedures are considered a term or condition of employment, collective bargaining agreements typically govern the procedures to some degree. The steps in progressive discipline involve, in this order, verbal warning, written warning, suspension without pay, and termination.

A verbal warning, sometimes referred to as "counseling," occurs during a private meeting between the supervisor and supervisee. At this meeting, the supervisor brings the problem to the supervisee's attention, describes the undesirable behavior or activity and its frequency and/or severity, clarifies the expected action or behavior for the supervisee, and attempts to gain a commitment from the supervisee to change the undesirable behavior. The supervisee has an opportunity to explain, ask questions, provide further information, or offer corrective solutions. The supervisor must inform the supervisee during the meeting of the consequences of not correcting the problem, that is, a written warning. Although the campus HR unit might consider verbal warnings informal and may not require them to be documented, warning meetings should be followed immediately with a short memo to the supervisee describing the problem discussed, the course of action necessary to correct the problem, and a deadline for improvement, for example, 30 days. This protects any future disciplinary action by documenting the verbal warning. In most cases, a written warning must have been preceded by a verbal warning.

A written warning is a memo from the supervisor to the supervisee whose performance has not improved as a result of the verbal warning

What is the best way to handle "difficult" employees?

Employees tend to be labeled "difficult" when certain behaviors are more frequent than the norm. Short of extreme disruptions or physical violence, the behaviors tend to be more aggravating than dangerous. When employees complain too much, exert too little effort, are absent or late too much, argue too much, need too many rationales for why something is important, need instructions repeated too many times, or request special treatment too often, the supervisor may view the employee as being difficult to supervise. Generally, these negative behaviors continue because they go unaddressed and can eventually raise or lower the norm for the entire work group. The approach is to coach first, and then use progressive discipline.

meeting. The memo summarizes the past actions leading up to the verbal warning meeting, specifies the current scope of the continuing problem(s), and specifies future disciplinary action that will result if performance does not improve immediately. Depending on the circumstances, disciplinary action to follow might include additional written warnings, suspension without pay, or termination. A written warning is carefully constructed, is highly specific, and uses formal language. The campus HR unit will have examples of written warnings and will help supervisors draft the warning memo. In many cases, written warnings may not be delivered until campus HR personnel have reviewed the contents. Written warnings should not be e-mailed to the supervisee; they should be hand-delivered in a sealed envelope at a discreet moment or sent with confirmation requested, such as certified or return-receipt mail. Further conversation about the warning memo should be limited to clarifying the contents rather than to defending or substantiating the contents of the memo, listening to additional reasons for noncompliance, or entertaining other information provided by the supervisee.

Suspension without pay can be a consequence of failure to comply with the performance improvements requested in a previous written warning and typically lasts from one to five days, depending on the severity of the problem and on collective bargaining agreements or state laws that govern suspension without pay. Because suspension without pay temporarily diminishes compensation, a collective bargaining agreement would almost certainly establish rules for such suspensions. Periods of three to five days are often reserved for serious issues, such as threatening another employee or a patron with harm, gross safety negligence, petty theft, or taking one or more days of absence without leave, or absence without request or notification (depending on the local regulations, longer absences may constitute "job abandonment," and the consequence can be immediate termination). Suspension without pay requires written notification, and the notification requires cooperation from campus HR, the payroll office, and designated union personnel if the employee is represented. The campus HR unit will have sample letters of suspension and a template for the letter, and it is important to follow the template strictly. Some of the content will cite state law or another regulation or the relevant article of a collective bargaining agreement that enables the suspension without pay. Some of the content will be provided by the supervisor, such as the past progressive disciplinary actions leading up to the suspension. As with the written warning, a letter of suspension without pay is hand-delivered or sent by certified or return-receipt mail.

Termination of employment is the ultimate step in progressive discipline, and no further opportunities for correction are available to the employee. There may be a review procedure available to the employee immediately before, or a grievance procedure immediately after, the dismissal, but these procedures only examine whether or not the disciplinary and dismissal processes were followed correctly and not the reason(s) for dismissal. Under some circumstances (depending on state law or collective bargaining agreements), the supervisor must send a notice of the intent to dismiss a supervisee on a certain date, and under other circumstances a dismissal letter can be sent without notice of intent. Dismissal letters always require the assistance, review, and approval of campus HR, and, if progressive discipline has been followed, HR personnel will be aware of the case history. Regardless of the egregiousness of a single offense (an employee physically attacks another person, reports to work intoxicated and/or is disruptive, etc.), the supervisor's immediate response is limited to sending the employee home or calling campus security to remove the employee and arrange for transport home or to a safe location. There is no such thing as on-the-spot dismissal by a supervisor acting alone.

Personnel Records and Retention

Personnel records, or a person's "personnel file," are variously defined by state statute and may be further specified by individual institutional policies and union agreements. Generally, personnel records include documents pertinent to a person's employment, for example, qualifications for employment and records of hiring, promotion, transfer, classification and compensation, disciplinary action, attendance, claims and grievance documents, and leave records. Some of these records may reside at the campus HR office, and/or in the library's administrative office, and/or at the payroll office. Supervisors may have copies of some of these documents in their desk or office files, but they are not responsible for maintaining official personnel files. Personnel records must not include personal information about health or medical care or personal financial information. If this type of information has been provided to or authorized by the employee in relation to FMLA or workers' compensation benefits, or to meet a requirement at hire, this information must be kept in files separated from personnel records. Documents that an employee has not seen or has not been offered a copy of should not be included in personnel files. Personnel records are confidential documents and, short of a court order or other legal process, are never provided to external parties.

An employee may have a right to examine his or her own personnel records, but there is no federal law guaranteeing this right. Employee access to personnel files is governed by state law, and those laws may differentiate between public and private employees. Even when there is no state law to establish a legal right to access, colleges and universities may establish the right through their own policies. Personnel records should be kept in locked files and may not be removed from the immediate area for examination; this prevents loss or tampering. Because it could be broadly interpreted, and has been argued, that any personnel information about an employee, regardless of its location, constitutes a part of the entire personnel record, supervisors should think carefully about keeping personal notes or records regarding supervisees in their work files. Something as small as a hastily written notation on the desk calendar, a draft version of a performance evaluation, notes about a job applicant, or an angry note that was never sent could come back to haunt the supervisor. If it is useful for the supervisor to write self-reminders or document what the memory so often fails to record, then these notes should be kept in a personal journal that is not stored at the office. This practice helps exclude a super-

How do I know if I have a right to see my personnel file?

Depending on state law and institutional policy, employees may or may not have a right to examine their personnel files. Some states have established the right for all employees; others for public employees only. Institutional policy may extend this right to employees, and collective bargaining agreements may include a provision that allows employees access to their individual personnel files. CanMyBossDoThat, an independent, nonprofit organization, maintains a useful state-by-state searchable database of employees' rights, including the right to see personnel files, at http://canmyboss dothat.com/category.php?id=281.

visor's personal notes from being considered part of an employee's personnel record.

Campus HR, along with other internal units like payroll, academic affairs, the EEO office, and the institution's records management unit are charged with the responsibility of compliance with a myriad of record retention requirements. Virtually every federal and state statute that involves any aspect of employment requires record keeping and establishes a retention period for the related records. Personnel documents retained in library administration may generally be considered "working copies" of official records for retention purposes. This is another situation in which cooperation with the campus HR unit can be invaluable—HR can't retain records if the library never sent them on, and the library can't verify past personnel actions if HR doesn't have a complete official record.

Summary

Becoming an excellent supervisor requires a conscious effort to develop and improve basic supervisory skills over time. The basic supervisory skill set includes expert knowledge of a library process, function, or service and the abilities to communicate effectively, to solve problems, and to motivate and coach staff members. Aside from the intrinsic rewards of mastering the supervisory role, it is in the supervisor's best interest to become effective in the role—the more a supervisor can develop the skill and performance of supervisees, the easier the supervisor's job becomes. At the other end of the spectrum, toxic supervision extinguishes any motivation supervisees might have had to contribute to the organization, damages staff and the organization, and hurts people unnecessarily. Until all employees are afforded legal protection from a hostile workplace, institutions should create strict zero-tolerance policies against workplace bullying. Among other duties, supervisors are responsible for carrying out the performance evaluation process required by the institution and for initiating and following through on progressive disciplinary processes. The next chapter discusses at length the performance evaluation system for library faculty and librarians with continuous appointment.

REFERENCES

Anonymous. 2010. *Rate Your Boss* (blog), December 28. RateYours.com. www.rateyours.com/a110/Rate-your-Boss-Boss-Ratings.html.

Buckingham, Marcus, and Donald O. Clifton. 2001. *Now, Discover Your Strengths.* New York: Simon & Schuster.

Cannon, Walter B. 1927. "The James-Lange Theory of Emotion: A Critical Examination and an Alternative Theory." *American Journal of Psychology* 39: 106–124.

Csikszentmihalyi, Mihaly. 1975. *Beyond Boredom and Anxiety: Experiencing Flow in Work and Play.* San Francisco: Jossey-Bass.

Namie, Gary, and Ruth Namie. 2004. "Workplace Bullying: How to Address America's Silent Epidemic." *Employee Rights and Employment Policy Journal* 8, no. 2: 315–333.

National Center for Education Statistics. 2011. "Academic Libraries: 2010, First Look." U.S. Department of Education. http://nces.ed.gov/pubs2012/2012365.pdf.

Rock, David. 2008. "SCARF: A Brain-Based Model for Collaborating and Influencing Others." *NeuroLeadership Journal* 1: 44–52.

Taylor, Frederick. 1911. *The Principles of Scientific Management.* New York: Harper and Row.

recruitments and search committees

Recruitment is the process through which potential employees are solicited, screened, evaluated, and recommended for hire. Although the specific rules for recruitment may vary depending on the status of the position being hired, along with who performs each step in the recruitment, the process follows a basic series of steps for most types of positions. Steps in recruitment include planning the position, gaining authorization to recruit, announcing and advertising the position, screening applicants and selecting the best qualified candidates, interviewing and assessing the final candidates, checking references and credentials, prioritizing candidates, extending an offer, waiting for acceptance, and then hiring the new employee.

For faculty and professional library positions exempt from the Fair Labor Standards Act, a formal search committee may be created and empowered to perform the recruitment steps involving selection and recommendation of one or more desirable candidates. For positions subject to the Fair Labor Standards Act, which are "nonexempt" positions (also called classified, paraprofessional, career-banded, merit, or support staff positions), a person designated the "hiring manager," such as the person who supervises the position or heads the department, will interview and assess preselected candidates and make a hiring recommendation to library administration and campus HR. The recruitment process for part-time, temporary student employees is generally handled by the immediate supervisor and follows an abbreviated or expedited process.

In general, recruitment processes and subsequent hiring decisions are considered management functions and are not mandatory subjects of collective bargaining. However, collective bargaining agreements frequently contain provisions to promote the advancement of current employees into vacancies rather than filling positions from the outside. Some agreements may include a "union shop" provision, which requires employees to belong to or pay dues to the union as a condition of employment.

History and Philosophy

During roughly the same period labor began to organize in the 1930s and through the 1938 passage of the Fair Labor Standards Act, most individual states had moved from a spoils system of hiring to a merit system of hiring; that is, rather than the ruling party simply awarding jobs to supporters and friends, jobs were given to the best qualified applicant based on objective measures of skills and abilities required to perform the tasks of a job. The creation of "civil service" in the states followed a federal civil service reform movement that began in the late nineteenth century. Public employees were openly and competitively recruited from a wide pool of interested and qualified job seekers. States established offices or departments of personnel administration to control the employment of "civil" or "public" servants, and these agencies were often overseen by an independent board. State civil service rules generally do not apply to exempted positions or to employees covered by a collective bargaining agreement. However, the principles of fairness in recruitment—openly posting and widely advertising position vacancies that define the knowledge, skills, and abilities required of applicants; evaluating the relative merits of applicants; and selecting the successful candidate based on objective assessments—are basic to every search.

Faculty and Professional Position Searches

Positions become vacant when the incumbent resigns, retires, or is otherwise separated from the library. A position vacancy is an opportunity to revise, reshape, or explore a new function or service, and many academic libraries pause at this point to refine or redeploy the position. This requires drafting a new position description and/or announcement. A formal position description can be used as the basis for an announcement, and sometimes the announcement is considered the actual position description. Either can be used as the basis for advertisements, and the terms "announcement" and "advertisement" are often used interchangeably, but advertisement generally implies the paid inclusion of vacancy information in a publication. Because positions "belong" to the institution first, and then to the library, but not to a department or functional group, permission to recruit must be gained from the academic division leadership and library leadership in order to initiate a recruitment. This step may be pro forma or may require a written request and justification for retaining the position. Most often, the vacancy must be documented prior to asking for permission to recruit—that is, assuming a position is to be filled due to a resignation or retirement, the incumbent must submit written notice of his or her intention to vacate the position on a specific date—the last working day. The position is still not considered vacant until the incumbent has left the payroll, that is, all paid leave days accrued by the incumbent have been expended. For example, if the incumbent has two weeks of paid leave on the last working day, the incumbent remains on the payroll for two weeks, plus the amount of leave time accrued during that two-week period.

PLANNING THE POSITION

Planning the position and requesting authorization to hire can be done simultaneously, and in the best cases planning has been underway prior to the date the position is vacated. Although not limited to periods of vacancy, the optimal time to revise or redeploy a position is when it is vacant. In difficult economic times, every position is expected to maximize the library's ability to deliver service, and only occasionally is a hire intended to replicate the previous position, to simply replace "what we had before" with "another one of them." Strategic questions about the role of a position and the rationales for asking might include these:

- Where in the library is the greatest potential or existing need for expansion? Consider building on existing strengths or opportunities versus emphasizing workload-driven decisions.
- Is the position expected to solve a librarywide problem or take lead responsibility for exploring a new service or function? Consider the level of specialization required and the need to pioneer new territory versus maintaining the status quo.
- Is the position expected to optimize or transform an ongoing function? Consider leadership and project management experience and skills versus strictly technical skills.
- Will the position be at a generalist level or a more specialized level? Consider the possibility of freeing existing specialized personnel from generalist duties and turning them toward higher level activities, leaving the generalist duties to create an entry-level, and less expensive, position.
- Will responsibilities of several jobs be combined into a single position or involve cross-functional work? Consider the potential for overloading a new person with too many, or conflicting, tasks or reporting to more than a single supervisor.

Planning the position's organizational location within the library, the scope and nature of position responsibilities, and the suggested rank or level of the position are generally determined by library leadership, often in consultation with department or functional unit supervisors or a faculty advisory body to the library's dean or director. Assuming authorization to fill the vacancy is received, the library's leadership group or the supervisor of the position can write a draft position announcement. The task also can be delegated to the search committee, but this is less efficient and less reliable in terms of interpersonal communication, and it can delay the entire search process. The clearer and more coherent the focus of the position, and the more descriptive the announcement, the more likely the announcement will be to attract a qualified applicant pool.

DRAFTING THE ANNOUNCEMENT

The draft position announcement should include the job title, a description of the role and specific duties of the position, the position's reporting line (the supervisor of the position), and the minimum qualifications for education, experience, knowledge, skills, and abilities. Applications from those who do not possess the minimum qualifications must be screened out (disqualified), so the minimum qualifications should be written to narrow or widen the potential applicant pool as appropriate to the position. Preferred qualifications are just that—qualifications that would advance one applicant over another. If no applicant meets any of the additional preferred qualifications, the search proceeds to consider the pool of applicants who meet the minimum required qualifications. All qualification statements must be job related.

Using descriptive terms in job titles or announcement text, such as "entry-level," "associate," "assistant," "senior," "coordinator," or "generalist," will help potential applicants to determine their own suitability. Avoiding overemphasis on personality characteristics, or terms that could be interpreted as exclusory or vague in meaning, such as "strong," "energetic," "dynamic," or "creative," is recommended. Descriptive terms may be dispositions that are desired in a successful candidate, but such dispositions may not always be easy to assess. When overused, these descriptors also may create an unintentional impression that, as a group, current library staff lack these traits altogether or that the last person in the position lacked these traits. At times the descriptors may even suggest gender or age preferences. Desirable characteristics are better expressed as prior experiences that would predict successful job performance, for example, specific leadership experiences, project management experiences, or previous career achievements that would demonstrate an applicant's capabilities.

For library faculty positions, expectations for achieving tenure or continuous appointment are generally included in an announcement (scholarship and service), along with information about the time frame for screening, for example, "screening begins on . . . and will continue until the position is filled" or "closing date is . . ." A "screening begins" date notifies interested parties that the committee will begin to examine applications completed by the specified date. A "closing date" indicates that applications received after the closing date, or applications that are not complete on the closing date, will not be considered. Positions that are open "until filled" indicates that the search will be active until a successful candidate is hired. Providing screening and closing dates or leaving the time frame indefinite provides a clue as to the urgency of the search time line. In a fair and open search, applicants must have adequate opportunity to see the announcement and a reasonable amount of time to respond with a completed application. Some applicants may not be intentionally in the market for a new job but may be attracted by a desirable posting and need time to gather the required documents or to contact potential references.

The substance of the final draft of the position announcement is usually fitted into a template provided by the campus HR unit, and this ensures consistent descriptive language, inclusion of information required by the institution, and inclusion of an EEO statement. Such a template might include the college or university seal or logo, a vacancy number, a prepared description of the institution's desirable characteristics (e.g., enrollment and faculty size, Carnegie classification, details about the geographic and municipal location, cultural and recreational opportunities, and benefits), eligibility requirements to work in the United States, instructions on how to apply, and sometimes a minimum salary or a salary range.

Depending on local policy, salary statements may be vague—"salary dependent on qualifications and experience" or "commensurate with experience" or "salary is competitive." Sometimes there is no mention of salary at all. This may decrease the number of applicants, which is not a desired condition, but some institutions are hesitant to convey salary in public announcements because of the belief that it does not advantage the institution to do so—that it is an advantage only to applicants. The rationale may be that the astute applicant will have looked up the salary scale, grid, or matrix on the institution's website to determine the salary potential before applying. Posting a salary range may encourage the successful candidate to start negotiation at or near the top of the range or to be insulted if offered the minimum or an amount close to it.

Knowing that current employees often watch the salaries listed in announcements, the institution may wish to avoid creating resentment, especially if salary compression has been a problem. Salary compression is created over time when conditions in the employment market cause salaries to rise, for example, the cost of living increases, the currency inflates, or certain skills are in higher demand than they were previously or are so new that few people possess them. This means that for similar positions, recent hires might be paid the same, or close to the same, as those hired earlier. When compression advances unchecked and reaches a point where recent hires are making more than earlier hires, this is called salary "inversion." Institutions may try to correct salary scales prior to compression/inversion by reindexing salaries, but it takes time to do so and the institution may not wish to advertise the problem.

Another rationale for including the vague "salary dependent on qualifications and experience" may be that the position has fewer required qualifications than preferred qualifications, and salary will be negotiated based on what the individual brings in terms of preferred qualifications and previous experience. This can be especially true for higher level positions in which the successful candidate is not expected to need a long training and development period or the need is so urgent that there is no time to wait for a person with potential to "grow into" a position. As policy, some institutions may require a statement such as "position contingent upon funding" to be included in the announcement. In reality, funding for a position has been identified during the search authorization process, but such statements offer a defensible position if something unexpected happens to prevent continuous funding, such as legislative or other reductions in future funding or budget shortfalls during the current year.

Statements such as "[college or university name] is an E-Verify Employer" indicate that the successful candidate's legal work status will be checked through the Department of Homeland Security in addition to completing the I-9 form, which is required for all new hires—U.S. citizens as well as non-U.S. citizens. The I-9 form certifies that a representative of the hiring employer has personally inspected the new employee's eligibility document(s) and identifies which documents were presented. Non-U.S. citizens who are eligible to work in the United States have what is popularly referred to as a "green card," which indicates that a person has permanent resident status. An H-1B visa allows an employer to hire a non-U.S. citizen to work for a maximum of six years, and the six-year period is sometimes used to pursue permanent residency. Some institutions embrace international hiring, most often for specialized high-need disciplines, and some do not. Some advertisements may contain a statement such as "[college or university name] will not sponsor individuals for employment," meaning that the institution will not hire and then sponsor an individual for H-1B status. This is not an exclusory or restrictive policy. Sponsorship can be a six-year process that can cost the employee thousands of dollars in legal fees, may involve multiple family members, and offers no real guarantee that the employee will gain permanent residency before the visa expires. When an H-1B visa expires in the sixth year, the visa holder must return to his or her home country. Whatever the institution's policy is on international hiring, it will have to be followed. If a qualification is modified in the announcement, such as "ALA-accredited degree *or international equivalent*," and the announcement is absent any statement regarding legal eligibility, this may mislead potential applicants to believe sponsorship is a possibility.

Once the announcement is approved by the academic and HR authorities, it should be distributed as widely as possible. Some institutions have subscriptions or membership arrangements for posting to well-known national websites, such as HigherEdJobs.com or the *Chronicle of Higher Education*, but library administration or the search committee members should also take advantage of relevant professional electronic discussion lists or blogs to distribute the announcement to targeted audiences. Posting the announcement on the library's website is also a useful practice both to solicit external applicants and to keep library staff informed of vacancies. Once the announcement is approved, the contents should not be edited before further distribution. If a shortened version is required, it should contain a link to the full text of the announcement.

SERVICE ON A FACULTY OR PROFESSIONAL SEARCH COMMITTEE

Unless otherwise prohibited by a faculty code, academic regulation, or union agreement, any employee may serve on a search committee. Search committees can be formed by election, appointment, or a combination of both. Members can include persons external to the library, library faculty or professional staff, and nonexempt staff. The search committee's job is to produce a successful search and recommend the best qualified candidate(s) to the "hiring authority," usually the library director or dean.

Search committees are typically on the small side, with three to five voting members, and may include an additional nonvoting member or two who bring special expertise or insight. Nonvoting members can include a representative of a constituency group or a related discipline and, if appropriate, students. The search committee's ultimate product is a recommendation(s) that will be passed upward to the next level for review and approval. Search committees do not make decisions; they make recommendations.

The committee may receive a charge that specifies the task and the time line, along with the position description or announcement. At the initial meeting, the committee elects a chair, reviews the charge and the announcement, and may be briefed by or asked to review written materials developed by the diversity officer. This provides an opportunity to remind or instruct search committee members on rules to ensure fair consideration of all qualified applicants, illustrate appropriate and inappropriate interview questions, and review the EEO process required to validate the search results.

Once the announcement has been distributed and advertised, the committee has a chair to coordinate the committee's schedule and activities, and the guidelines for a fair search have been reviewed, the next task is to develop a matrix or scoring rubric for screening applications. The matrix should contain a checklist of the required qualifications. This section will be used to screen out any applicants who do not possess the required qualifications. No applicant who lacks these qualifications would be considered further, with the possible exception of degree completion by the anticipated start date, so there is no benefit to completing the rest of the scoring matrix or rubric. Another section of the rubric should include the preferred qualifications, which may be weighted by their relative importance, and differentiated by the suitability or quality expressed in the application and related materials, such as a Likert-type scale from 5 to 1 (5 being highest) or "high," "medium," and "low" corresponding to 3, 2, and 1, in terms of points. The total score would be used to rank applicants from highest to lowest. For example, if the position announcement invites applicants who have excellent communication skills, then the letter of interest and any publications would be an initial indicator of written communication skills that could be included on a screening matrix.

Screening the Applications

Most institutions now have an online application facility, and these are called "applicant tracking systems." Applicants are asked to complete forms online and upload required documents. The major advantages of these systems are to reduce paper handling and loss, ensure privacy of applicants' personal information, expedite the screening process, provide 24/7 accessibility to committee members and applicants, and enable the aggregation of management information useful in improving the search process. When an application is complete, the tracking system may send an automatic e-mail to thank the applicant for completing the process. Search committee members have password access to the application folders and can check for and fill out the screening rubric for completed applications either online or on paper. Some tracking systems have the capability to sort applicants by different levels, roughly equivalent to "good, better, best," based on totals from committee members' individual matrix ratings. When the closing date or the "screening begins" date is reached, the evaluation and screening process should proceed without delay. The chair should call a meeting to discuss applicant rankings, select applicants to interview, schedule possible dates for telephone and/or on-site interviews, develop a structured list of interview questions, and notify the appropriate library administrative personnel of the committee's progress. Applicants who did not meet the required qualifications should be sent letters of declination at this time. Applicants who met the required qualifications but were not selected for further consideration also may be notified at this time. Some search committees may not consider this a strategic move, and, depending on the pool, it may not be wise to dismiss other applicants at this stage of the search. There is always the possibility that the most qualified applicants will be unavailable to interview, will decline an invitation to interview, or will have accepted another position before they are contacted. However, it is a courteous practice not to keep applicants hanging any longer than necessary, especially if the search committee is not strongly positive about their qualifications.

Interviewing Candidates

When an applicant has been selected for interview, he or she is then referred to as a "candidate." If the number of desirable candidates exceeds three, or the library has a number that it considers the appropriate or maximum number to invite for on-site interviews, the field can be narrowed by conducting short interviews by telephone or some type of web conferencing tool. Telephone or online interviews are subject to the same EEO guidelines as on-site interviews and should employ a structured set of questions to be asked of each person. The committee should prepare from five to seven open-ended questions, and the interview should take no more than an hour to complete. Be sure to allow time at the end of the interview to solicit and answer questions from interviewees. Because telephone/web interviewing adds a step to the process, interviews should be scheduled as quickly and as tightly together as possible.

There are various styles of interviewing, but one style thought to be particularly effective is behavioral or behavior-based interviewing. Behavioral interview questions ask interviewees to give specific examples of past behaviors that may be future predictors of job success. For example, rather than asking a candidate to enumerate his or her strengths or weaknesses, candidates are asked to illustrate their skills and abilities with examples. Most behavioral questions begin with the phrase "Can you tell us about a time . . ." or "Can you give us an example of . . .":

What topics are not permissible for inquiry during an interview?

Federal law prohibits asking questions that relate to the following candidate characteristics:

- Gender and family matters (marital status, living arrangements, children, child-care arrangements, spouse's occupation, etc.)

- Race, national origin, or ancestry (race, ethnic association of surname, native language, how the applicant learned to speak English, place of birth, etc.)

- Religion or religious practices (holidays observed, manner of dress or clothing, food restrictions observed, etc.) unless a bona fide occupational qualification (For example, if the employer is a college or university connected to a church organization, there may be a reasonable hiring preference for persons who hold the same or similar religious beliefs.)

- Disability or health issues (nature or severity of disability, history of workers' compensation claims, current health, past injuries, etc.)

- Military service or discharge status other than specific and related military work experiences included on the candidate's résumé

- When you were in a situation where you had to adjust to changes over which you had no control? How did you manage that situation?
- When you were able to convince someone from outside your department to cooperate with you on an important project? How did you begin to gain the person's support?
- Some people consider themselves to be "big picture people" and others consider themselves to be "detail oriented." Which are you? Can you give an example of a time when you demonstrated this?
- Tell us about some things you have done to become more effective in the positions you've held in the past?
- How do you go about gathering or developing enough information to make important decisions? Have these means been effective in the past?
- In your previous or current position, how did you go about establishing yourself within the library, making key contacts, and beginning to create the relationships necessary for you to succeed?

Not all the interview questions have to be behavioral, as these can be somewhat intimidating, especially if delivered in rapid sequence or if they constitute the entirety of the interview. Although there are no right or wrong answers to behavior interview questions, search committee members should have some idea beforehand of the kinds of answers they are looking for in terms of depth and analysis and should be ready to rate the response on a scale of one to five or to assign some numeric score. Asking other questions about specific job experiences that the candidate is proud of, projects accomplished, or achievements related to the duties of the position and the candidate's area of expertise offers a chance for the individual to shine and make a good impression on the search committee. As directed by the EEO officer during committee briefing, or in the materials or instruction provided to search committee members, all questions asked of interviewees should be job related.

Most libraries already have a well-developed agenda for on-site interviews that features meetings with the departmental work group and the search committee, the dean or director, and the supervisor of the position and a presentation on a preassigned topic or issue and/or an open question-and-answer period for the faculty and staff at-large. Tours of the library and the campus and one or more opportunities to socialize with faculty and staff are usually included on the agenda. Interview duties for search committee members may involve picking up a candidate from the airport and taking him or her to the previously arranged hotel, taking a candidate to lunch and dinner, conducting the library and campus tours, escorting the candidate from meeting to meeting, lending whatever assistance the candidate may need while a guest of the library, and seeing the candidate safely back to the airport. Near or at the end of the interview, the candidate should meet with the search chair or the library dean or director to bring closure to the interview and to ask the candidate for his or her impressions of the library and the position. If the candidate has any reservations about the position, perceives any barrier to accepting a possible offer, or has any questions that he or she may have considered inappropriate to ask in a group situation, the interviewer can help resolve these issues for the candidate. Being candid and encouraging during this meeting may increase the likelihood of a positive response to an offer. Every candidate should be treated as if he or she were the first-choice candidate.

Like telephone or online interviews, on-site interviews should be scheduled as quickly and tightly together as possible. Many a desirable candidate has been lost because a search has moved slowly and the candidate has accepted another offer. Candidates should be told the time line for the remaining steps in the search process and when they might expect to hear something back from the library. They should be kept informed of any changes to the time line, and, if the time between interview and expected offer is longer than one month, the search committee chair should touch base with each candidate, even if it is simply to communicate that the process is continuing. This contact with each candidate should be brief, factual, and restricted to information on the status of the search. It is not unheard of that hiring can be frozen even after campus interviews have been conducted. Maintaining contact to reassure candidates that the search is still in process will help build trust and confidence between a potential employee and the library and may make the candidate more likely to accept an offer if and when it does come.

Checking References

Most instructions to potential applicants ask interested parties to provide three or more reference contacts and later may require three or more written letters or e-mails of reference prior to hire. Checking references is a crucial step in the process, and it should not be rushed through or approached as the final hurdle to get to the recommendation stage. Reference checks are often performed by the search chair, but they can be delegated among the committee members or performed by the person who will supervise the position. Reference providers can be extremely useful to confirm the search committee's appraisal of the candidate and to provide insight into the candidate's past work experience, work habits, or accomplishments. They can also help to eliminate a candidate who has not been strictly accurate about statements made during interviews or about previous educational or work experiences. This is not to say that candidates make less than truthful statements but that people have different perspectives on past events, and vantage points may differ. For example, if the search committee allows a candidate to remain the "best qualified" despite considerable information from reference providers to indicate otherwise, then the merit basis of the search loses integrity and may even lead to a regrettable recommendation. If the reference-checking process reveals discrepancies among reference providers or between their accounts and those of the candidate, then additional reference providers may need to be contacted.

Besides reference checks, what other kind of checking should normally be made prior to hire?

Institutions should always check employees' educational credentials. For jobs that require a postsecondary degree, official transcripts are normally required prior to hire. The job may require a degree from a college or university that is regionally accredited, and the Council for Higher Education Accreditation maintains a searchable database of recognized institutions and programs at www.chea.org/search, with links to each associated regional accrediting body. For a job requiring completion of a degree from an ALA-accredited program, use the Office for Accreditation's historical list of accredited programs at www.ala.org/accreditedprograms/directory/historicallist. Providing false information about credentials to an institution, especially if they are required qualifications for a position, may result in immediate dismissal. Some institutions require criminal background checks for all employees, but few require credit checks or drug testing.

There are several ways to perform or delegate reference checks, depending on the normal practice followed by a library. Some search committees may wish to check references for all candidates who have been invited to campus, for the first-choice candidate only, or for two front-runners. Even though it is implied in the application process that references will be checked, it is courteous to inform candidates prior to doing so, and it can save time and effort if the candidate has decided that the library is not his or her first-choice employer or has accepted another offer. If a candidate has not provided the current supervisor as a reference because the candidate wishes not to disclose that he or she is looking for another job, then the candidate should be notified before contacting the supervisor. If for one reason or another, reference providers are unavailable or decline to participate, the candidate should be asked for additional reference contacts. It is also permissible to ask one reference provider for the names of others who are able to speak directly to the candidate's qualifications, but, as a courtesy, the candidate should be notified prior to contacting any second-party reference providers. The search committee has a legitimate need to know information about a candidate's work history and work performance but not to "go fishing." This would be unethical and is not likely to build trust with potential employees. The genuinely prepared candidate is willing to help the search committee bring forward a positive recommendation, and cooperation in this part of the process indicates authentic interest in the position and the library.

Speaking to reference providers is a specialized form of interviewing, and, like telephone and on-campus interviews, the conversation should follow a set of structured questions asked of each reference provider. Early questions should be factual in nature (e.g., clarify circumstances under which the provider knows or knew the candidate and how long they have known the candidate, verify length of previous or current employment and the position held) and move to more evaluative questions about the candidate's past performance and competencies. Final questions can address the candidate's developmental needs and solicit comments or suggestions for the new supervisor. Examples of typical reference-checking questions include the following:

- How would you characterize the candidate's work style?
- What do you consider some of the candidate's professional strengths? Could you provide an example or two?

- What do you consider some of the candidate's professional limitations? Could you provide an example or two?
- Could you describe a recent job-related challenge that the candidate faced and how he or she responded?
- Do you have firsthand knowledge of how the candidate behaved in a stressful or uncomfortable work situation? Could you provide an example or two?
- What is your perception of the candidate's ability to work successfully and effectively with a variety of people (students, teaching faculty, library colleagues, vendors, administrators, parents or other campus visitors, etc.)?
- How would you characterize the candidate's work ethic?
- Is or was your library or organization better off by having employed this person? In what ways? Could you describe the cumulative impact the candidate had on your organization?
- Do you have any suggestions for the candidate's further training and development?
- Do you have any suggestions for the candidate's potential new supervisor as to the management style that would be most effective for him or her?
- If given the opportunity, would you hire the candidate again? Why or why not?
- In conclusion, is there any other job-related information you would like to add regarding this candidate?

The reference checker(s) may take notes, but, as with telephone and campus interviews, responses should rated numerically. A Likert-type scale, or another scale similar to the one used for rating telephone and on-campus interviews, should be used for reference checks. If references have been checked for more than one candidate, this data, along with the interview ratings, should be used to rank the final candidates in order. Ranking all acceptable candidates by numeric scores helps a search committee remain unbiased and documents the committee's experiences and impressions as they occurred rather than relying on the committee's collective memory. This allows the library a fall-back position if the search committee's recommendation is adjusted at higher administrative levels. In some cases search committee recommendations are forwarded to a library personnel committee for confirmation, then by the personnel committee to the library dean or director, and then by the library dean or director to the chief academic officer or his or her delegate. Search committees do not make decisions; they make recommendations to the hiring authority.

Making a Recommendation

Having gathered additional information from reference providers, the search committee may meet for a final discussion to decide which candidate, or how many candidates, to recommend and in what rank order. Committee members may be tempted to languish at this stage, especially if there was no "perfect" candidate. Conversations about the "fit" with the library should be restricted to job-related requirements or avoided altogether. "Fit" is an elusive quality that can mean anything from "we liked this candidate best because he or she was the most like us" to "this candidate had the high level of interpersonal communication skills that will be necessary to work in a position with librarywide impact." If "fit" can be defined by knowledge, skills, or abilities, then the discussion becomes transparent and defensible. If not, then it may be an indulgence in the pleasures of speculation.

On the other end of the spectrum, the committee may be tempted to rush their recommendation or to recommend a mediocre candidate just to bring the search to closure. It is natural to feel some fatigue at this stage of the process, but the chair should remind the members of the initial purpose of the recruitment—to identify the best qualified candidate(s) and the candidate(s) with the greatest potential to contribute toward achieving the library's mission and fulfilling the immediate goals of the position. If it is the committee's firm belief that no candidate is well qualified or has the potential to be successful in the position, then the recommendation must be to close the search or ask permission to continue or reopen the search. The committee's recommendation should be clear and emphatic, and it should be delivered in writing by the chair to the appropriate individual who will carry it forward to the next administrative level. In cases when governance is specified in a written faculty code, manual, or constitution, the recommendation may be made to the chair of a library personnel committee. This committee may agree or disagree with the search committee's recommendation and may pass along an altogether different recommendation to the authorized hiring official.

ADMINISTRATIVE REVIEW OF SEARCH COMMITTEE RECOMMENDATIONS

After the search committee has made a recommendation, it will take a period of time for the recommendation to be confirmed at higher administrative levels, and the committee is not dissolved at this point but waits for further action. It is extremely important for committee members to remain silent during this period of latency. Library colleagues will be interested to know the results of the search and will ask committee members which candidates, if any, were recommended. It is advisable to respond only with information about the status of the search process, for example, the committee has made a recommendation to the personnel committee or to the director, the committee's recommendation is under review by the EEO officer at campus HR, and so forth. If the names of successful or unsuccessful candidates are leaked, this information can travel quickly to the candidate or the candidate's current library colleagues. This can be embarrassing to the candidate, who may not have shared his or her availability for the position with coworkers and may disadvantage the negotiating position of the hiring official who will make the offer. It is embarrassing for the library if unsuccessful candidates learn about their status through the grapevine before the library has had a chance to send a courteous letter of declination. In the worst case, the committee's recommendation may not be confirmed at higher administrative levels, and the information about successful or unsuccessful candidates may no longer be accurate as represented by committee members.

As soon as the recommendation has been formulated, the search committee chair should prepare the EEO forms provided by campus HR to "certify" the search. The certification review verifies and records that the search followed correct procedures and resulted in a defensible recommendation. These forms typically ask for information on the number of qualified applicants, the number and names of candidates interviewed by telephone and/or on campus, the name of the recommended candidate and the reason(s) for selection, and the reason(s) unsuccessful candidates were eliminated from consideration. Depending on local requirements, the search chair may also be asked to compile and report the numeric scores from the matrices used for screening applications and evaluating interviews and reference checks. If there is a discrepancy between numeric scores and the search results, these will need to be explained in detail, for example, "candidate withdrew from further consideration after telephone interview." Handwritten notes referring to specific candidates should be destroyed at this time. This is a recommended practice because notes or marginalia on forms become difficult to interpret as time passes and are difficult for others to interpret accurately. This protects the candidates, the library, and the institution. A notation as simple as "funny guy" written in the margin can mean the candidate exhibited a good sense of humor, or the committee member thought the candidate behaved oddly, or perhaps was in some way "funny looking." Notations innocently made to help a committee member recall a specific person, such as "wore that great looking suit" or "the short one," can be interpreted later as reflecting a personal bias.

OFFER OF CONTRACT FOR EMPLOYMENT

Once the recommendation has been confirmed at intervening administrative levels (personnel committee, campus HR, the library dean or director, and the provost/chief academic officer or his or her delegate), the "hiring official," who is the person with the authority to hire, will contact the candidate to make a verbal offer. Depending on local practice, the hiring official can be the president or chancellor, the provost/chief academic officer or a designated associate at this level of the organization, or the library dean or director. Most often, hiring authority is delegated to the library dean or director. The designated official makes a verbal offer to the successful candidate at a suggested annual starting salary, identifies the desired start date, and may discuss incoming rank, length of probationary period if there is flexibility (e.g., credit for previous years served), possible subsidization for moving expenses, and any other benefits that might be available. The goal of making an offer is acceptance, and the hiring official will do everything possible to "sell" the college or university and its library to the successful candidate. This may involve several conversations to come to acceptable terms for both parties and, in the case of professorial rank or credit toward tenure, may require a confirming faculty vote. In consultation with search committee members and the library dean or director, the search chair may send letters of declination to candidates who were interviewed on campus but not recommended as the first-choice candidate. It may be wise to wait and see if the offer is accepted by the first-choice candidate, and, if not, then an offer can be made to the next-ranked candidate.

At the time a verbal offer is accepted, the hiring official should ask the individual's permission to announce the hire. This allows the incoming employee to submit a resignation and prepare to transition between employers. It also allows the hiring official to prepare a letter of offer, sometimes called the contract letter, for the appropriate administrator's signature. The offer letter contains the terms and conditions of employment negotiated by the hiring official and those required by the institution. Most likely, this letter is prepared by the hiring official for signature by the provost/chief academic officer or the president/chancellor. The offer letter will be reviewed prior to signature to ensure that contract terms are accurate, and any errors must be corrected before the letter is signed and sent. The signed letter is sent to the incoming employee, who countersigns a copy and returns it to the sender. The offer letter may include an expiration date or a period of time in which the signed copy must be returned, such as 30 days, for the offer to remain valid.

At some point during the offer and acceptance process, the search committee is released, committee members are thanked for their service, and the committee dissolved. It is rare for an individual who has signed a contract letter to renege, but it does happen on occasion. It is most likely that the search has been concluded and the vacancy closed, so a new recruitment would begin and the original search committee could be reconstituted or a new committee formed. Depending on the timing of events, there may be the possibility of going back to the candidate pool and making an offer to the second-ranked candidate. The decision rests on how much time has elapsed and whether the second-ranked candidate is still available. Considering the time and effort that goes into a search, and the good fortune of having more than one desirable candidate, it may be advisable to pursue this action. It takes sensitivity and consideration for another person's feelings to explain the situation to the candidate, but the offer of a job is flattering no matter when it arrives and will be appreciated regardless of the circumstances.

Nonexempt or Classified Staff Recruitments

Nonexempt positions are those subject to the Fair Labor Standards Act and are referred to variously as classified, paraprofessional, career, graded or banded, merit, or support staff positions. In publicly supported institutions, employment transactions for these positions are regulated by federal and state law and may be further subject to a collective bargaining agreement. In independent institutions, these positions are subject to federal law and any applicable state law and also may be subject to a collective bargaining agreement.

In publicly supported institutions, these employees are employees of the state first and then employees of the institution and its library. That is, most aspects of employment are governed by state civil service laws, and there is less flexibility in hiring than for exempt employees, but the hiring process follows most of the same steps to ensure fair and open searches designed to hire the best qualified candidates. Hiring non-exempt staff members is a joint and collaborative effort between the library and campus HR, and maintaining clear and open communication throughout the process will assist in achieving a successful result. Private institutions may have somewhat greater latitude in recruitment and hiring procedures and may have fewer internal levels of review and control, but they are subject to the state and federal laws that apply to recruitment and hiring.

Announcements or position "postings" are developed from a set of specifications determined at the state level, which will include knowledge, skills, and abilities qualifications determined by the state's personnel authority as appropriate to the duties of the position. This set of specifications will determine the pay grade or pay band of individual positions. Typically, vacancies are announced by the state through postings to a website, are searchable by job title and location, and offer an online application facility. The university system, individual system institutions, and their libraries may make additional postings or collaborate with the state personnel authority to interlink their postings. Announcements may be advertised in local newspapers or other paid distributors at the discretion of the institution and its library and may be distributed through related professional electronic discussion lists and professional associations or agencies, such as state library job sites. Rather than "open recruitments," which solicit applications year-round for many vacancies statewide, most library job vacancies have a closing date after which no further applications will be taken.

Immediately after the closing date, the state personnel authority will begin to review applications. This task may be delegated to campus HR to perform, and campus HR may ask for library input, but the library will not control the process designed to develop a "register" or a list of qualified applicants for consideration by the library hiring manager. The list may be ranked or unranked and, if there are many applications, may be limited to the highest ranked, for example, ten or more if there are ties in rankings. There may be regulations for the number of applicants to be interviewed, for example, at least two from the five highest ranked.

Ranking protocols will delete applicants who do not meet the minimum education, experience, knowledge, skills, and abilities qualifications specified for the position. Remaining applications will be evaluated by comparing the applicant's qualifications with the duty specifications for the position classification and any specific examples of appropriate duties provided by the library. The ranking protocol may also take special or priority considerations into account, and these considerations can include applicants who have "career" or permanent status in the same classification series—for example, those who are presently working in the same classification and are seeking lateral transfer; those who are presently working in a lower classification in a series and are seeking promotion; those who have been either of the above but have lost their jobs due to a reduction in force; and those who are returning to work after being on workers' compensation leave. Special consideration may also be extended to eligible veterans. The register is conveyed to the hiring manager, along with paper forms or a password to online forms that will document the search results. Individuals who are not on the register or certified list of qualified applicants may not be interviewed and therefore cannot be hired. There are no exceptions to this rule.

The hiring manager, who is usually the supervisor and/or leader of the department, will contact individuals to arrange interviews, and they may conduct the interviews either alone or with job or departmental peers in all or some portion of the interview. Interviewees should be asked a structured set of questions, just as for exempt positions. It is the hiring manager's responsibility to select the successful candidate and check references, but he or she may gather input from others at his or her discretion. When the selection process is completed, the hiring manager prepares an EEO summary and submits it to campus HR, along with a request to hire. If a background check is required, campus HR will initiate the proper procedure.

When the request to hire is approved and the pay grade and salary are identified, the offer can be made and a start date negotiated. Campus HR may make the offer or may delegate authority to the library hiring manager to do so.

Student Employee Recruitments

Students are yet another status category of employees and can be either hourly wage earners (e.g., paid a straight hourly wage through financial aid programs, such as federal or state work-study programs or from library funds) or contractual employees (e.g., undergraduate or graduate assistants who receive a salary or stipend and work on a time-limited contract). In all cases, student employees are temporary, part-time employees and, by definition, are not eligible for permanent or continuous employment status. Their employment is at-will, meaning they can be dismissed at any time, and they can resign at any time.

Student employment is mutually beneficial to the student and to the library. Employment on campus provides students with a means to offset the cost of higher education and to gain work experience in a setting conducive to their academic success. Without student employees, academic libraries would have difficulty covering all their service points and locations during open hours. Student employees extend and supplement the work of full-time employees.

Wage earning students are hired and can be rehired each semester or quarter, and salaried students may be hired for as long as an academic year. Because the library is expected to fund, or to coordinate funding that subsidizes, the costs, authorization from higher levels is normally not required prior to recruitment. Position announcements can be regulated by individual campus policies and procedures but are not subject to the same controls exerted by campus HR or academic authorities for full-time permanent positions (e.g., assignment of a unique position number, review and approval of announcements, external dissemination of announcements, and approval prior to offer). For these positions, hiring authority is delegated to the library.

Many colleges and universities have student employment offices that post online job vacancies for all campus employers, and these announcements can be supplemented by posting flyers in the library and residence halls or handed out at the circulation desk. Some libraries have periodic recruiting fairs for students, and current student employees often encourage their friends to apply for jobs in the library.

Students fill out application forms, either on paper or online, and the hiring manager (usually the library staff member who will supervise the student) reviews applications and contacts selected students to arrange interviews. Selection decisions are normally made by the supervisor or the supervisor in consultation with staff and/or a library HR authority. Applications may be screened using a matrix, but they are most often evaluated based on student interest and prior work experience and availability to work during the days and times required. Offers are normally made by phone or e-mail. When students are hired, they must complete paperwork to verify their enrollment status and eligibility to work in the United States, to certify their tax liability (W-2 withholding allowance form), and to sign some type of personnel action form, which will be used to enter information to the payroll system.

Some institutions have very well-developed policies for student employment that include job classification levels, pay scales, and performance evaluation systems. Some are less formal and leave these issues to the discretion of the hiring unit. However, colleges and universities will recommend or require as a condition of financial aid that students work no more than 20 hours a week when class is in session, maintain a minimum GPA, and be registered for a minimum number of credit hours. If these conditions are not met (e.g., the student drops courses or withdraws), then the student's employment is terminated. Although student employment is at-will, some campuses have courtesy policies to encourage employers of students to provide notice prior to termination and to encourage student employees to provide notice of resignation, and they may suggest methods for handling student employee grievances.

Summary

Recruitment is the process through which potential employees are solicited, screened, evaluated, and recommended for hire. Filling a position vacancy through recruitment requires joint effort and coordination among individuals and campus units in order to complete a series of steps in a manner that is timely and that complies with federal and state regulations, as well as institutional policy. Because a library's personnel *are* the library, recruiting is the initial and perhaps most important process through which a library builds and renews itself. It involves making recommendations or decisions about the library's greatest overall expenditure—recurring salary, wage, benefits, and development costs. Good recruitments reduce turnover, increase job satisfaction and productivity, and enable the library to achieve its mission and goals.

RECOMMENDED READING

Association of College and Research Libraries. 2004. "A Guideline for the Screening and Appointment of Academic Librarians Using a Search Committee." American Library Association. www.ala.org/acrl/standards/screenapguide.

Association of College and Research Libraries Ad Hoc Task Force on Recruitment and Retention Issues. 2002. *Recruitment, Retention and Restructuring: Human Resources in Academic Libraries*. Chicago: American Library Association.

Engel, Debra, and Sarah Robbins. 2009. "Telephone Interviewing Practices within Academic Libraries." *Journal of Academic Librarianship* 35, no. 2: 143–151.

Fitsimmons, Gary. 2010. "Directing the Personnel Search Part I: The Position Announcement." *The Bottom Line: Managing Library Finances* 23, no. 4: 205–207.

———. 2011. "Directing the Personnel Search Part II: Notes on Contacting Applicants." *The Bottom Line: Managing Library Finances* 24, no. 1: 38–40.

———. 2011. "Directing the Personnel Search Part III: Preliminary Interviews." *The Bottom Line: Managing Library Finances* 24, no 2: 110–112.

———. 2011. "Directing the Personnel Search Part IV: The On-Site Interview." *The Bottom Line: Managing Library Finances* 24, no. 3: 157–159.

Gilreath, Charles L., Christine L. Foster, Leslie J. Reynolds, and Sandra L. Tucker. 2009. "Lessons Learned by a Standing Search Committee: Developing Better Practices." *Journal of Academic Librarianship* 35, no. 4: 367–372.

Hazelton, Penny A. 2011. "Practical Tips for Academic Employers." *AALL Spectrum* 16, no. 2: 12–14.

Kenney, Donald J., and Frances O. Painter. 1995. "Recruiting, Hiring, and Assessing Student Workers in Academic Libraries." *Journal of Library Administration* 21, no. 3–4: 29–45.

Meekins, Cynthia. 2012. "NSEA Principles of Professional Practice." National Student Employment Association. Accessed June 2. www.nsea.info/docs/about/governing/NSEA_PrinciplesOfProfessionalPractice.pdf.

Raschke, Gregory K. 2003. "Hiring and Recruitment Practices in Academic Libraries: Problems and Solutions." *portal: Libraries and the Academy* 3, no. 1: 53–67.

Stevens, Jen, and Rosemary Streatfeild. 2003. *SPEC Kit 276: Recruitment and Retention.* Washington, DC: Association of Research Libraries.

U.S. Merit Systems Protection Board. 2005. "Reference Checking in Federal Hiring: Making the Call." U.S. Merit Systems Protection Board. www.mspb.gov/netsearch/viewdocs.aspx?docnumber=224106&version=224325&application=ACROBAT.

tenure and continuous employment

Despite mixed feelings toward tenure expressed throughout the library literature, the practice of awarding tenure or continuous employment status to librarians is widespread in academe. This chapter discusses the general process and specific procedures commonly adopted by institutions and their libraries in making point-in-time retention decisions about individual librarians. Although the chapter is intended as background for those who serve on promotion and tenure committees, it is also useful for tenure-track librarians, library administrators, and anyone who is interested in learning more about tenure and continuous appointment. Topics include the role of the promotion and tenure committee, guidelines and criteria for promotion and tenure, contents and construction of a personnel dossier, reviewing and evaluating dossiers, and general best practices for promotion and tenure evaluation.

Foundation and Philosophy

The basic purpose of tenure or similar assurance of continuous employment is to provide a reasonable expectation of continued employment and protection against unfair dismissal. Perhaps the signal event in the development of tenure in the United States was the dismissal of the economist Edward Ross from Stanford University in 1900. Jane Stanford, widow of railroad magnate Leland Stanford, Sr., and cofounder of the University, remained heavily involved in its operation until her death. She did not like Ross's views on race, immigrant labor, and railroad monopolies, and he was dismissed for this reason. By 1913, the American Economic Association, the American Political Science Association, and the American Sociological Society formed a joint committee to study and report on at least 11 different complaints of unfair faculty dismissals and group resignations in protest of dismissals. In 1915, John Dewey and Arthur O. Lovejoy organized a meeting to form an association that would work to ensure academic freedom for faculty. This group became the American Association of University Professors and the same year published a "Declaration of Principles on Academic Freedom and Academic Tenure." In part, this declaration stated:

> Definition of Tenure of Office. In every institution there should be an unequivocal understanding as to the term of each appointment; and the tenure of professorships and associate professorships, and of all positions above the grade of instructor after ten years of service, should be permanent (subject to the provisions hereinafter given for removal upon charges). In those state universities which are legally incapable of making contracts for more than a limited period, the governing boards should announce their policy with respect to the presumption of reappointment in the several classes of position, and such announcements, though not legally enforceable, should be regarded as morally binding. No university teacher of any rank should, except in cases of grave moral delinquency, receive notice of dismissal or of refusal of reappointment, later than three months before the close of any academic year, and in the case of teachers above the grade of instructor, one year's notice should be given. (American Association of University Professors, 1915)

Additional points of the Declaration addressed the need for institutions to formulate and make clear the grounds for charges leading to dismissal and the judicial process necessary to ensure a "fair trial on those charges before a special or permanent judicial committee chosen by the faculty senate or council, or by the faculty at large." Tenure in the present day evolved from three basic principles in the Declaration: faculty should be protected against dismissal for communicating or espousing unpopular ideas; cause for dismissal should be reviewed and judged by a "jury of peers," so to speak; and faculty should be given adequate notice of nonreappointment.

Defining Tenure (Continuous Appointment)

For the purpose of simplicity, "tenure" will be used to refer to any process designed to provide an expectation of continuous appointment to faculty who have successfully completed the probationary period. The Association for College and Research Libraries (2010) provides this definition of tenure:

> Tenure, or continuous appointment, is defined as an institutional commitment to permanent employment to be terminated only for adequate cause (for example, incompetence, malfeasance, mental or physical disability, bona fide financial exigency) and only after due process.

The University of Nebraska–Lincoln Libraries (2007) describes the roles of both parties in the tenure agreement, emphasizing that tenure is a mutual commitment among the University, the library, and the faculty member:

> The Libraries commits to support the work of the faculty member throughout her or his career. The faculty member commits to continue to grow as a professional and a scholar-practitioner and to contribute significantly to the goals of the University, Libraries, and the profession. . . . Continuous appointment is the most significant reward that the University can bestow on a faculty member.

Consortium Library (2010: 6), which serves the University of Alaska Anchorage and the Alaska Pacific University, explains the primary purpose of tenure being "to assure the academic community of an environment that will nurture academic freedom by providing employment security to faculty members, as well as faculty continuity to the University."

■

What exactly does a collective bargaining agreement look like?

They are special types of contracts between an employer and a group of employees who are represented by a union, and they cover issues including wages and fringe benefits, grievance procedures, arbitration, health and safety, nondiscrimination, no-strike clauses, length of contract, discipline, and seniority. Management rights include determining the mission, budget, and organizational strategy and may include numbers and types of personnel to be employed, as well as any issues not specifically negotiated in the agreement.

The Office of Labor-Management Standards in the Department of Labor maintains a searchable database of collective bargaining agreements and makes it available to the general public for information and study purposes at www.dol.gov/olms/regs/compliance/cba.

Generally speaking, tenure in unionized environments is similar to tenure in nonunionized environments, but there is a great deal of variation due to the nature of collective bargaining, state employment laws, and judicial interpretation. Sun and Permuth (2007) studied 30 years of cases involving unionized faculty evaluations (for tenure, promotion, and annual review) and illustrated the complexities of more recent cases at length and in detail. Separating issues of faculty evaluation into the academic or educational domain (managerial and outside the scope of bargaining) or into the employment domain (terms and conditions of employment and within the scope of bargaining) has been challenging. Some state courts have ruled that criteria for reappointment, tenure, and promotion fall under the "other terms and conditions of employment" in bargaining agreements and were open for negotiation. Other rulings have held that faculty evaluation is inherently managerial in nature and not open for negotiation (Sun and Permuth, 2007: 119–121).

In making this distinction for faculty evaluation when members are represented by a union, the general rule of thumb considers two factors. The first factor is the substantive evaluation criteria, that is, the requirements for tenure in terms of job performance, scholarship and service, and the threshold level for meeting these requirements. In the absence of collective bargaining or law that provides otherwise, these are academic (managerial) decisions. This managerial decision-making process begins with the promotion and tenure committee's recommendation for or against the award of tenure and higher rank, which will be sent upward to management—the library dean or director, a universitywide review committee, the provost, the president or chancellor, and the board of trustees or regents. Depending on the size and culture of the institution, there may be a single campuswide tenure committee or a library tenure committee, or both. These committees make recommendations for consideration by administrators, for example, the library dean or director, the provost, and a governing body (trustees or regents). The review process flows upward from the lower unit to higher levels.

The second factor is the implementation of procedures for faculty evaluation, or for providing "due process," and the process and procedures are more often considered to be terms and conditions of employment. Faculty tenure committees and all the parties involved in the process chain (the candidate, the library dean or director, university level reviewers, the provost, etc.) must follow *exactly*, and in sequence, the procedures proscribed by the system (if applicable), a collective bargaining agreement (if applicable), the institution, and the library for the conduct of tenure reviews. These procedural matters include meeting deadlines and following fixed schedules of events, filing the proper forms and notices, complying with voting procedures, overseeing the inclusion and exclusion of evidence in the evaluation file or "dossier," and following procedures to identify and select external reviewers.

Role of the Library Promotion and Tenure Committee

The tenure committee consists of tenured faculty composed in a manner proscribed by a governance document such as a faculty manual, code, or constitution. The tenure committee may be a "committee of the whole," consisting of all tenured faculty members, or a smaller number of members elected by the tenured faculty of the library. The tenure committee may also act as a promotion committee to make recommendations regarding promotion to Associate Professor or an equivalent, such as Librarian III or Associate Librarian. Promotion and tenure may be considered by an institution to be separate administrative actions or a single concurrent action. When considered separate actions, there are two committees—one to make the tenure recommendation and another to make the promotion recommendation. When there are separate committees, depending on the size of a faculty and the tenure status of the faculty members, the membership of the tenure committee and the promotion committee may not be identical. A separate promotion committee is constituted to make recommendations to the highest rank—Professor or an equivalent, such as Librarian IV or Librarian. For the purpose of clarity, promotion and tenure will be discussed as a single personnel transaction and the library promotion and tenure committee referred to as "the Committee."

In an effort to avoid tie votes, the Committee size is sometimes specified as an odd number of members. It is a standing Committee and typically works year-round, regardless of the number of probationary faculty members scheduled for final tenure review. The Committee will elect a chair, usually the most senior faculty member or the faculty member with the most Committee experience, who will direct the Committee, keep reviews on schedule, and ensure compliance with guidelines. The Committee is also involved in interim reviews of faculty due for reappointment (e.g., annually or at years two and four or three and five); participates in developing progress-toward-tenure evaluations; reviews materials; and makes recommendations for incoming faculty who have requested tenure or rank at the time of hire. The Committee should be involved regularly in working with junior faculty to assist with development and preparation of the evaluation file or dossier. Similar to a portfolio, the dossier is a collection of evidence composed of specified documents arranged according to a set of guidelines. Dossiers are also referred to as "promotion and tenure packages [or packets]" or "personnel action files." The Committee's most important task is to review candidates' dossiers and make recommendations regarding the award of tenure and promotion in rank.

Guidelines for Promotion and Tenure

Guidelines for the tenure and promotion process(es) are published in a faculty manual, code, or constitution that has been developed through a system of faculty self-governance. There may be layers of guidelines at the system, institution, and library levels, and guidelines from the level below cannot contradict or conflict with guidelines from the level above. That is, the library can create its own set of guidelines, but it cannot create guidelines that conflict with the institution's or the system's guidelines. In general, these guidelines include:

- a clear description of the procedures that will be followed, including a timetable and deadlines for each step or stage of the process;
- the criteria for tenure and for each successive rank and expectations for librarians regarding tenure and promotion in rank;
- eligibility to serve on the Committee, how members are identified or convened, length of the term of service, and a Committee rotation schedule;
- a statement concerning the confidential nature of Committee deliberations;
- Committee voting procedures, the number of "yes" votes required, and how abstentions and absentee ballots will be handled;
- a listing of contents of the dossier and instructions for dossier preparation;
- procedures to handle unusual or unexpected events (In the best cases, promotion and tenure guidelines have established procedures to deal with adding or updating dossier contents during the review process, for example, recently submitted or accepted publications, completion certificates from professional development activities, honors/awards, and so forth. Other useful procedures might address disagreements over the inclusion or exclusion of documents between the Committee and the candidate, dealing with unsolicited comments from faculty who are not Committee members, and procedures for replacing a Committee member who needs to step off or wishes to recuse himself or herself from deliberation and recommendation.);
- requirements for the identification and selection of external reviewers; and
- instructions on how the Committee's recommendation is to be prepared and conveyed to the candidate and the library dean or director.

What is post-tenure review?

Post-tenure review is an umbrella term for the widespread practice of performing comprehensive, cumulative, and multiple-year performance evaluations of tenured faculty members. In the more common form, such reviews are designed to examine evidence across three to seven years of work performance and productivity, adding a layer of longer-term evaluation to the annual review process. In this process, every tenured faculty member is reviewed periodically. Less used is a process wherein post-tenure reviews are triggered automatically after a set number of unsatisfactory annual reviews or unsatisfactory performance on a single or multiple criteria across time. The purposes of post-tenure review are to allow for examination of longer-term outputs and performance over time for summative evaluation and to establish a reliable mechanism to institute formative professional development to improve job performance. Post-tenure reviews often require the preparation of a modified dossier that undergoes peer and administrative review. If deficiencies or consistently unsatisfactory performance are revealed in librarianship, research and creative activity, or service, the faculty member and the library dean or director develop a performance improvement plan. Progress is tracked at specific intervals, and a time limit is set for completion of the plan.

Many academic libraries have developed tenure and promotion guidelines that serve as excellent examples for study, and they provide insight into the variety of processes, methods, and criteria for promotion and tenure. For the Committee's most important task—making recommendations on candidates' tenure and promotion—it is critical to have a firm command of the stated criteria and a clear sense of the threshold levels for meeting those criteria.

Criteria for Promotion and Tenure

The criteria for promotion and tenure are deceptively simple: teaching and/or librarianship (job performance), research and creative activity, and service. In practice, evaluating a librarian's contributions along the criteria and across a five-year probationary period is no easy task. Unlike teaching faculty, whose workloads are relatively well controlled by departmental assignments, such as the number of courses taught and student credit hours produced, the librarian's workload is somewhat resistant to measurement and evaluation by a uniform rubric. In some libraries, it's possible that no two librarians have exactly the same responsibilities or set of duties, making it more difficult to compare individuals against an established performance standard. Despite the variety and divergence of library work, there are implied or expressed expectations for competence, productivity, and professional commitment.

JOB PERFORMANCE

The criteria adopted by an institution for its teaching faculty are at variance with the librarian's role, and although job performance may include instructional or teaching activities, the teaching role and criteria are always reinvented or interpreted to describe the job role and job performance for academic librarians. The Coates Library at Trinity University makes this clear in its criteria for tenure and promotion:

> In other words, librarianship will be considered as a related but different category of activity from teaching. Librarians will be evaluated on the quality of their librarianship in all of its appropriate facets, not on whether librarians model the teaching activities of other faculty. Implementation of computer systems and original cataloging of materials, for example, should both be based on priorities that consider the effects on our users and their academic success. Additionally, it is expected that librarians will demonstrate strong abilities as generalists, able to perform effectively in a variety of tasks and, often, a variety of departmental disciplines as selectors, reference experts, and information literacy instructors. (Coates Library, 2012: 2)

Excellence in the performance of professional responsibilities is, without exception, the first requirement for tenure and promotion of librarians. A review of criteria statements regarding job performance from many library faculty manuals makes this quite clear. Job performance is identified as the first criteria listed in guidelines for tenure and promotion. These are some example statements that recognize the primacy of job performance:

> Library faculty must have at least notable job performance to be considered for promotion and tenure. Notable job performance indicates that the individual candidate has a sustained record of surpassing the merely satisfactory level of job performance. (Louisiana State University Libraries, 2006: 6)

A librarian must, first and foremost, excel in the position held at Indiana University. (Indiana University Libraries, 2010: 21)

Teaching/Librarianship: The library and its faculty are central to the teaching and research mission of the University. In evaluating Library faculty, teaching/librarianship encompasses the basic work responsibilities of a librarian or archivist. (Consortium Library, 2010: 1)

While librarians are expected to demonstrate achievement in all areas, the librarian's primary workload focus is librarianship. Furthermore, within librarianship, greatest weight is to be given to a candidate's performance of his or her primary responsibilities as indicated in his or her job description. (Boise State University Libraries, 2011: 3)

The quality of the performance of a library faculty member in carrying out his/her primary responsibility is always the chief criterion for evaluation. (American University Library, 2011: 1)

Job performance or librarianship is the defining criteria, and when job performance does not meet the standard, whatever it may be, the review should not result in a positive recommendation. When the job performance criterion is well defined and clearly understood and the evidence of excellence is compelling, then the reviewers' task is easier.

Unfortunately, not every case suggests a straightforward decision. Job performance may have varied across the first five probationary years, or there may be conflicting opinions or evidence to document job performance. The candidate may have served in more than one position during the probationary period, or may have been reassigned to responsibilities not in the original position description, or may have failed to document the progression of responsibilities. The greater the level of articulation and specificity required for job performance in the library's written guidelines for tenure and promotion, the easier it is for a candidate to document, and the easier it is for reviewers to arrive at a recommendation. From a review of numerous library faculty guidelines for promotion and tenure, suggestions for increasing the clarity of expectations for job performance are to:

- include express statements of performance behaviors and characteristics that may be implied, such as collegiality, teamwork, cooperation, communication, ethics, and core values;
- include a brief discussion of how changes in major responsibilities
or internal reassignments during the probationary period should
be presented and explained;
- provide numerous examples of evidence or assessments that
should be included either within the dossier or in a companion
portfolio;
- state any expectation for evidence of progression, or demonstra-
tion of a pattern of growth in the work record across the probationary period, as opposed to an expectation for a stable and sustained record of work performance across years;
- when possible, describe core workload expectations for both the
amount and quality of work; and
- clearly explain differences among job performance, service to
the library, and outreach activities. This explanation, along with
instructions to candidates not to include accomplishments under
more than one criterion, can help candidates parse out the distinc-
tions and prepare a more effective dossier.

Some guidelines for promotion and tenure may specify the percent-
ages assigned to each criterion, for example, 70–80 percent for job performance, 15–20 percent for research and creative activity, and 15–20
percent for service. Some guidelines may split criteria into separate categories, such as dividing service into service to the profession, service to
the institution and the library, and service or outreach to the community.
Guidelines may describe professional development activities that include
continuing education through workshops, attendance at professional
conferences, or advanced professional preparation (coursework beyond
the initial library credential).

RESEARCH AND CREATIVE ACTIVITY
The overarching criterion for research and creative activity may be
defined in library guidelines by broader terms such as "scholarship" and
"professional contributions." Describing exact expectations for quantity,
quality, and focus of scholarship for librarians has proven to be a difficult
task. Within a single library organization, especially in large research uni-

versities, librarians often engage in a wider variety of intellectual pursuit and expression than teaching faculty, who are organized into disciplinary departments. It becomes difficult to compare research across library promotion and tenure candidates because it is likely to run the gamut from qualitative to quantitative to nonempirical and may include critique, expert opinion, or presentation and performance venues. There may not be a single metric to permit exact comparisons of the scholarly products generated by all library faculty members, but guidelines for scholarship should be broad enough in scope and deep enough in detail to capture the essential elements. The University of Illinois Library and the Penn State University Libraries both provide guidelines for research and creative activity that describe the desired *outcomes* of scholarship. Although both documents provide examples of the types of products that result in successful scholarship, they avoid conveying an impression of scholarship as a dish for which there is a universal recipe. The University of Illinois Library makes its expectations clear in this concise statement:

> A candidate's scholarly and creative work shall be evaluated in terms of its originality, depth, and significance in the field. There should be evidence that the faculty member has been continuously and effectively engaged in scholarly activity of high quality and significance. . . . The Committees shall consider the type, scope, and impact of the research or other creative work, and consider both the evidence offered by the candidate and that solicited by their members from external referees at other research universities. (University Library, 2008)

Penn State University Libraries also describes scholarship as a process resulting in a desired outcome rather than suggesting a rubric for evaluation:

> A faculty member of the University Libraries is expected to establish and sustain a program of high quality research and creative accomplishments appropriate to his or her core responsibilities and rank which are consistent with the Libraries' mission and goals. . . . The scholarship of research and creative accomplishments is documented through a portfolio of quality accomplishments, reflecting an active and focused research program. (Penn State University Libraries, 2010)

There are many paths to achieve the desired outcomes for research and creative activity, and each candidate for promotion and tenure selects his or her own path. When quality indicators are difficult to identify and apply consistently, candidates and reviewers alike tend to fall back on quantity as the more important measure and may even obsess over "how much is enough" or what "counts" toward promotion and tenure. There are reports in the literature attempting to identify and compare significant publication venues specifically for application to faculty promotion and tenure processes. Nisonger and Davis (2005) surveyed directors of member libraries of the Association of Research Libraries and asked them to rank a list of library and information science journals by prestige and found that the top five were *College & Research Libraries, Library Trends, Journal of Academic Librarianship, Library Quarterly,* and *Reference & User Services Quarterly.* Other studies have compiled lists of possible considerations for evaluating publications, and these have included publisher's reputation, length and number of references, journal impact factors, citation counts, positive reviews from book selectors or external reviewers, and even library holdings data for books and monographs. Amazingly, no reports appear to suggest that members of promotion and tenure committees should themselves read, view, or use the scholarly product as a valuable way to estimate quality. East Carolina University's Academic Library Services' (2003) criteria for faculty evaluation hint at this, noting simply that "Ultimately, the [Committee] reviewers must make a determination on the significance of any activity reported."

From a review of numerous library faculty guidelines for promotion and tenure, suggestions for increasing the clarity of expectations for scholarship include the following:

- When examples of acceptable scholarly publications are listed, indicate a clear hierarchy among the types of publications listed when there is a preference, or group types of publications or products in the order of their relative significance.
- If grant applications or awards are considered scholarship, make a clear distinction between service grants and research grants, if such a distinction is recognized.
- Clarify if coauthorship carries less than, equal to, or greater weight than sole authorship.

- Suggest the appropriate subject focus for scholarly activities and any limitations on, or preferences for, scholarship relevant to the candidate's work role, library and information science in general, and disciplines other than library and information science.
- Clarify the appropriate category for participation on review boards and jury panels and editorships, that is, whether these activities are considered professional service or scholarship and how they can be distinguished.
- State the time frame of interest for scholarship. Folk wisdom suggests that for tenure, only those products written or created, submitted, or published during the probationary period should be considered but that for promotion, a candidate's lifetime record of scholarship should be considered.

The evaluation of research and creative activity generates perhaps the greatest anxiety among candidates and can be the most time-consuming and difficult evaluative task for Committee members. Indiana University Libraries (2010: 21–22) provides a useful perspective and empowers reviewers to consider "the balanced case":

In *exceptional* cases, a librarian may be tenured or promoted based on excellent performance and a presentation of balanced strengths across the other two areas of professional development, research and/or creativity, and service. In such cases, where neither of these two areas reaches the appropriate level of distinction when considered separately, the consideration of the two areas together show a level of distinction appropriate to the rank under review. The balanced case may be particularly suitable for librarians whose professional development, research and/or creativity, and service activities are very closely intertwined. The balanced case (see UFC Circular U13-94) will not compromise current criteria for performance and may be applied only to professional development, research, and/or creativity and service.

The concept of the balanced case offers reviewers the opportunity to evaluate candidates in situations when the lines between job responsibilities, scholarship, and service may be indistinct or overlapping. For example, those with administrative, managerial, or librarywide responsibilities may find it difficult to distinguish between exceptional performance and service to the library. At some point, innovative and highly successful work accomplishments may transcend job performance and become service to the library. At some point, operational research reports or reports authored corporately on behalf of the library may resemble scholarship. At some point, widely used databases created by a systems librarian or a digital projects librarian may resemble scholarship. Setting the appropriate balancing point between the quality and usefulness of content and the method of scholarly distribution is ultimately up to the Committee and the subsequent reviewers at higher levels. If the library faculty's group philosophy is holistic, that is, it considers every contribution in each category toward the sum total of a candidate's merit, then holding a more traditional and separate mental scoring rubric for scholarship may not be useful. If the library faculty's group philosophy is atomistic, that is, more concerned with peer-reviewed products and their related indicators of quality than other products, then peer-reviewed journal articles are likely to be the "gold standard."

Regardless of the philosophical approach taken toward evaluating scholarship, the publication or dissemination dates of scholarly products will be important. For tenure consideration, publication dates are expected to fall within the candidate's probationary term. This helps to define the quantity of products and to measure scholarly output as part of a candidate's overall efficiency. As a general rule of thumb, a candidate's career-long record of scholarly output may be considered for promotion. The reasoning behind this principle is that the sponsoring college or university shares credit for the work produced by a faculty member, but the faculty member is the scholar. It is much more likely that a librarian's rank is portable to the next institution than his or her tenure. When leaving the institution, the only thing the librarian "owns" and takes away is his or her record of scholarship.

SERVICE

Service is a reflection of the candidate's citizenship in the library, the college or university, the profession, and the external community. For the most part, service can be considered to be any professional contribution a candidate has undertaken voluntarily rather than activities specified in his or her position description or that constitute a regular work assignment. Because librarianship is a service profession and relies on the collective efforts of many, library faculty often have well-established and distinguished records of service. The opportunities for professional service are well refined and available at state, regional, and national levels. In addition, library faculty have the same opportunities as teaching faculty to serve on unit, institutionwide, and faculty governance committees and to perform outreach service to the external community. Given these factors, it is not unusual for the library to have higher service expectations than what departments place on teaching faculty.

Is a tenure dossier part of the employee's official personnel file?

The short answer is that it probably is. Because the dossier has been compiled in support of an employment action (employee retention beyond the probationary period and/or promotion) and is given voluntarily to the employer, a part of or the entire dossier may be retained permanently or for a relatively long period of time. Some institutions retain the entire dossier, and some discard the supporting materials (copies of publications, philosophy statements, copies of certificates, etc.) and retain only the substantive material (the curriculum vitae and formal application for tenure and promotion forms, forms with signatures, external letters, etc.). If the entire dossier or parts of the dossier are retained, public access to these records and the information contained in them will be limited by state law.

Dossier Construction and Contents

Instructions for preparation of the candidate's dossier or "package" are developed at the system or institutional level and applied to all faculty candidates. This permits reviewers at the library and successive levels to find information quickly and in the same location across many dossiers, and the standardized reporting format increases transparency and enables fairness. By the final review for promotion and tenure, the candidate has received feedback and suggestions from the Committee on the structure and placement of documents and advice about the inclusion or exclusion of selected documents. Institutions may require a single dossier formatted for promotion and tenure review and another formatted for a promotion-only review. A table of contents may be required, along with tables of contents for each section. Although the contents and their sequence can vary, the following are typical sections and elements of a dossier for promotion and tenure.

PERSONNEL DOCUMENTATION

This section contains documents that track a candidate's history with the library and establish the candidate's eligibility for promotion and tenure. This section can include the candidate's letter of initial appointment and subsequent reappointment letters, annual evaluations from the supervisor(s), the candidate's annual goals and annual reports on goal attainment, progress toward tenure letters sent to the candidate by the director or dean, a signature page to be signed by the appropriate authority at each level of the review process, an executive summary or longer narrative prepared by the candidate making his or her case for tenure, a cumulative evaluation statement or letter of recommendation prepared by the library committee, and a recommendation letter from the dean or director.

COPY OF THE LIBRARY'S CRITERIA FOR PROMOTION AND TENURE

Somewhere near the front of the dossier, candidates may be asked to provide a copy of the library faculty guidelines that describe the criteria for promotion and tenure of librarians. This is a courtesy copy for reviewers at levels above the library who may not be intimately familiar with every campus unit's criteria for promotion and tenure.

COMPLETE CURRICULUM VITAE

This is the "centerpiece" of the dossier and distills the candidate's total contributions to the library and the institution into a concise listing of facts and provides a synopsis of one's professional career. The candidate may be required to follow a strictly formatted template or may be given written guidelines and/or examples to illustrate the suggested form for an acceptable curriculum vitae.

DOCUMENTATION OF JOB PERFORMANCE

This section may include the candidate's narrative history of accomplishments and innovations related to his or her job responsibilities, both as singular and team efforts. The candidate may be asked to include work samples, examples of reports or manuals, finding aids, instructional presentations and handouts, student and peer evaluations of instruction, and letters of appreciation or commendation from students and faculty.

The candidate may be asked to present a philosophy of librarianship and, if applicable, a teaching philosophy.

DOCUMENTATION OF SCHOLARSHIP

This section may require a bibliography of all publications and presentations, reprints or copies of published articles and book chapters, works accepted (along with letters of acceptance), works submitted, and works in progress. For book-length works, candidates are typically asked to include bibliographic information, a short abstract, and any published reviews of the work. Other evidence may include exhibit catalogs, bibliographies, translations, entries in reference works, letters to the editor published in a professional journal, columns written for research or practitioner journals, book or media reviews, technical reports, and grant proposals or reports. Creative activity can be documented by summary descriptions of and links to works such as a widely read professional blog site, digital exhibits, websites or pages, tutorials, webinars, and so forth. The candidate may be asked to present a philosophy of scholarship and/ or a future research agenda.

DOCUMENTATION OF SERVICE

Service activities are typically sorted and presented in order of the beneficiaries of a candidate's service, such as the library, the institution, the profession, and the external community. Professional service may also be ranked by the level of impact, for example, local or metropolitan, statewide, regional, and national professional organizations or societies, and whether the service position was appointed or elected. Service activities generally include serving on committees or task forces at all levels of impact, leadership positions on committees or tasks forces at all levels, working on special projects, participating in library self-studies or contributing toward program and regional accreditation studies, serving as an editor, reviewer, or referee when such activities are not otherwise considered scholarship, participating in conference planning, mentoring junior faculty, and presenting guest lectures or providing in-house or external training. Service as a requirement for promotion and tenure and the expectations for service are closely tied to the culture of a college or university. For example, institutions that have elected the additional Carnegie classification of "community engagement," or that are heavily involved in outreach to a community or region, may prize service more highly than others. Institutions affiliated with a religious denomination may prize church or denominational service or missionary work, because the church and the educational institution together can be viewed as a horizontal organization. Typically, but not always, appropriate service rests on extending one's professional expertise to external groups and/or representing the institution or the library in an official capacity. If the connection is not immediately clear to reviewers, it is the candidate's responsibility to explain the relationship.

OTHER PROFESSIONAL ACTIVITIES

Generally, there will be an opportunity in the curriculum vitae to list significant activities not specifically reserved to the job performance, scholarship, or service criterion, and there may be a separate section of the dossier to document these activities. Included in this section are professional development activities that impact job performance or competence (additional graduate coursework, workshops, continuing education, and seminars attended, etc.), honors, awards, recognitions, scholarships received, professional memberships, consulting, grant proposals and outcomes, invited workshops or lectures presented that do not fall under other categories, and licenses or certificates. A summary statement, along with documents or other evidence, may be required.

LETTERS FROM EXTERNAL REVIEWERS

This method of peer review provides Committee members and subsequent campus reviewers with an independent, unbiased appraisal of the quality and quantity of a candidate's contributions to the library and the profession. Materials sent to external reviewers often include the candidate's curriculum vitae, a summary statement developed by the candidate, the library's criteria for promotion and tenure, and examples of scholarly products, such as journal articles, book chapters, and other publications. These materials are sent to three to ten outside experts who have special knowledge in the candidate's area of expertise. In some cases, an additional, but smaller group of reviewer names may be solicited from within the library. The practice of including internal reviewers is more likely to be followed at large libraries than at medium or small libraries.

Names of potential external reviewers are submitted by the candidate and by the Committee to create a pool, for example, three to five names suggested by the candidate and an equal or greater number of names suggested by the Committee. Some institutions permit the candidate to identify reviewers they would not wish to be invited. Reviewers should represent peer institutions and already be at the rank sought by the candidate. They should be national or international experts in an equivalent field of academic librarianship. The Committee will make the final selection of external reviewers, and the library's administrative office will solicit the reviewers' participation and send a prepared package of materials to the reviewers.

Although the Committee will have provided feedback, suggestions, and corrections to dossier contents and construction during mid-probationary reviews, the onus for producing a complete dossier meeting the format requirements is on the candidate. Parker (2011: 210) offers this excellent advice to candidates:

> Candidates may be tempted to demonstrate creativity or invent a "better" way of delivering the material than has been used in the past. By doing this, however, they may unwittingly make the reviewers' work more difficult if needed information is buried in a mass of text or must be accessed through a novel organizational approach. Worse still is failing to directly address relevant performance review criteria in the material submitted. Reviewing committee members may not be generous enough to ask for additional information or give candidates an opportunity to clarify or supplement what was initially provided.

Reviewing and Evaluating the Candidate's Dossier

Officials at subsequent review levels will examine the dossier and will be influenced by the Committee's and the dean's or director's recommendations. It is ideal if the Committee adopts a process for evaluation that involves more than just examining the dossier and meeting to discuss the members' findings. Some agreement on the requirements for making a positive recommendation should be discussed and reached prior to reviewing candidates' dossiers. Committee members should be encouraged to compare candidates to the agreed-upon standard rather than compared to one another. This helps to minimize the essential subjectivity of the promotion and tenure judgment. After knowing the candidate for a number of years, Committee members are likely to have formed an opinion about his or her suitability for promotion and tenure. However, the recommendation must be made on the basis of the evidence, and reviewers at subsequent levels will expect the recommendation to match the evidence provided in the dossier.

Garnett S. Stokes (2012), Provost and Executive Vice President for Academic Affairs at Florida State University, offered this perspective on reviewing dossiers for promotion and tenure:

> Sometimes I have a sense that the earlier recommendations for tenure by the department and/or school or college have been of the "courtesy" type. That is, the individual was a very nice person who had worked hard and been a good citizen in the department, and the unpleasantness of a negative vote is an unhappy experience. Collegiality, and even personal friendship, are important, but they cannot stand alone and must be viewed in relation to performance of duties and fulfillment of the university mission.

Job performance should indicate a record of progress toward increased impact, outcomes, and significance of the candidate's work in fulfillment of the library's goals, and it should describe contributions made both as an individual and as a team member. It is impressive when narrative statements and related evidence demonstrate a candidate's enthusiasm for his or her work, or the discovery of a new area of interest that might benefit the library, in addition to the candidate's clear vision of a direction for his or her future contributions. The supervisor's performance evaluations should support or reinforce the candidate's documentation of productivity and quality in job performance. Multiple assessments from multiple sources should be in agreement. The supervisor's performance evaluations, the candidate's self-evaluation or reflective statements, documentation of projects or accomplishments, progress-toward-tenure letters, work samples, and so forth, should be in alignment. Job performance that meets or exceeds the library's standard is the first requirement for promotion and tenure. If the evidence is contradictory or inconsistent across time, a positive recommendation may not be in the best interests of the library.

The evaluation of scholarship should include any appropriate means of professional expression that are recognized within librarianship and should consider the quality and quantity of all scholarly products documented within the dossier. Appraisal from external reviewers should be given significant weight. The Committee (sometimes in consultation with the library director) selects those who will be invited to review a candidate's materials, presumably because these reviewers are recognized experts in the candidate's field of librarianship and because they are able to provide an unbiased appraisal of the candidate's professional status and scholarly products. To give anything less than full consideration to these external appraisals in the evaluation of a candidate's scholarship would not only be unfair but also would constitute a deviation from procedural guidelines, and it may establish a basis for later grievance.

A candidate's service record and record of continuous professional development may be somewhat easier for the Committee to evaluate, especially when the candidate has provided explanatory or contextual narrative to an entry in the curriculum vitae or reporting form. Major service venues and important professional associations are generally well known and understood within academic librarianship. It is also understood that important positions in national professional associations are rarely given to librarians who have recently entered the profession, so a progression toward national status and reputation may signify potential for future contributions. Despite the expectation for future growth, all candidates may be expected to demonstrate their attempts to serve by volunteering or self-nominating for service roles within the library, the institution, and the profession.

Best Practices in Tenure Evaluation

Being eligible to serve by virtue of their own tenure, and being willing to serve through election or automatic appointment, members of the Committee accept a dominant position of influence within the library. Over time, the Committee will help to shape the library faculty body by making recommendations on the retention or nonretention of probationary faculty. Committee members should follow, in all their separate and collective actions and communications, a set of principles that includes clarity, confidentiality, consistency, candor, and care. These principles and the following discussion are loosely based on suggestions presented by the American Council on Education (American Council on Education, American Association of University Professors, and United Educators Insurance Risk Retention Group, 2000).

CLARITY

Although Committee members are not often directly responsible for creating promotion and tenure policies or for writing administrative guidelines to govern the process, they are nonetheless responsible for ensuring that the tenure process and criteria are as clear and transparent as possible. Members should rely on the formal documents and any relevant institutional and library communications to explain policies and procedures. When there are questions without immediate answers, then the chair should consult those who are senior authorities on promotion and tenure (the provost's office, faculty senate office, library dean, or director). Committee members should be knowledgeable about the criteria and the process but should refrain from offering opinions directly to candidates without benefit of Committee discussion or outside the Committee's meetings with candidates. Candidates are concerned about their progress and prospects, especially during the deliberation process, and may press Committee members individually to seek reassurance or implied promises of support.

Committee members should not seek information on candidates outside the proscribed process and related procedures. That is to say, Committee members should not solicit the opinions of external parties, identify and use criteria other than those established in the guidelines for promotion and tenure, seek information or documents outside the dossier, or consider any previous experiences they may have had with the candidate prior to the probationary period.

CONFIDENTIALITY

Maintaining confidentiality is important to protect the candidate, external reviewers, and the Committee members, as well as the integrity of the entire process. Penn State University provides this explicit instruction to Committee members and candidates:

> Confidentiality of the promotion and tenure process is to be respected forever, not just during that particular year of review. Members of promotion and tenure committees participate with the understanding that all matters related to their deliberations remain confidential. In addition, faculty candidates under review are discouraged from approaching committee members at any time concerning the disposition of their review and should understand that inquiries of this type are deemed entirely inappropriate. (Office of the Vice Provost for Academic Affairs, 2009)

Policies protecting the confidentiality of external reviewers and the contents of external review letters vary from institution to institution. In some institutions, the names of the reviewers and the contents of the letter are never shared with the candidate or others outside the Committee and administrators in the review hierarchy. In others, reviewers are notified in the solicitation letter that candidates will have access to their review letters. Some states have laws that establish an employee's right to see documents in his or her personnel file, including external letters, and the entire dossier can be considered part of the personnel file. In other cases, a candidate may see the letters, or redacted letters (with identifying information blacked out), upon request or see them only when the review is complete.

The assurance of confidentiality protects all parties involved in the review. It protects the candidate from being the subject of misinformation and rumor during a long and anxiety-producing process. It permits the external reviewer to provide a genuine appraisal without fear of reprisal or negative consequences. It protects Committee members from being misquoted or misinterpreted, and it keeps Committee deliberations free from external influence. It protects administrators and others in the review hierarchy from situations that may be harmful to the library or the institution. Maintaining confidentiality demonstrates respect for all the parties involved, and it supports the basic integrity of the process.

CONSISTENCY

Consistency in process and in application of the stated criteria across multiple reviews can be challenging, but it is essential to ensure fairness. Committees make individual recommendations based on a candidate's merit compared to a merit standard but, over time, leave a record of evaluation that allows comparison among many candidates. From a legal standpoint, consistency is a great concern at all levels of review. Unsubstantiated differences in a pattern of reviews, or final recommendations at variance with a candidate's annual evaluations of progress toward tenure, or recommendations that appear to have cut the cloth to fit an individual, so to speak, may be considered "disparate treatment." Disparate treatment is the essence of the claim of discrimination. Aside from the general improvement of decisions that results from vetting candidates at all levels in the academic organization, these multiple levels of review promote fairness and help ensure a degree of consistency across candidates in many disciplines, across candidates in the same year, and across candidates in several years.

Consistency at the library level of review may be enhanced by establishing longer terms for Committee members, for example, four to six years, and a rotation schedule that ensures stability in Committee composition across time. If one or more members of the Committee are also experts in a candidate's area of expertise, the Committee chair should take care to correct for the possible tendency of these members to set a higher standard for the candidate than they might for other candidates. Recommendations should be based entirely on the contents of the dossier. External factors such as a candidate's "fit" within the library or likability can be considered a bonus, but they are not a valid basis for recommendation. Likewise, a candidate's unfortunate personal circumstances can be viewed with sympathy, but the candidate's personal needs are not a valid basis for recommendation.

CANDOR

By the time of final review, the candidate and the Committee have met several times regarding the candidate's progress toward tenure and have discussed performance on each of the criteria. The candidate has met periodically, if not annually, with the library director or dean, perhaps with the chair of the Committee present, to discuss progress. The candidate will have received letters documenting his or her progress, noting both achievements and areas for improvement, along with specific examples of how progress might be demonstrated. By the time of final review, there should be no question as to whether or not the candidate will be recommended for promotion and tenure. Candor during earlier probationary reviews is an interpersonal and professional responsibility. If a probationary faculty member has not shown promise along the way, or is unwilling or unable to improve, then waiting until the final review to address the problem is not a favor to the candidate. If the candidate has not been explicitly and repeatedly made aware of deficits in job performance, scholarship, or service, then neither the Committee nor the library dean or director has acted ethically. Few enjoy delivering criticism, and few like to be criticized. All feedback, including bad news, is a gift to the candidate but only if it is received in time to do something about it.

CARE

Committee members have two responsibilities of care. The first is to deliberate with care—or to take the care a reasonable person would exercise when making recommendations about a candidate's future employment. Committee members should study the relevant governance documents of the library and the institution regarding promotion and tenure processes and procedures, attend every Committee meeting, make themselves available to probationary faculty who have questions about the process, and devote adequate time to the study of candidates' dossiers.

The second responsibility is to care for candidates throughout the process. No one goes through the promotion and tenure process untouched. There may have been many disappointments during the course of the probationary period—accepting and responding to negative feedback, coping with a set of standards imposed by those who may not be perceived as having met the standards themselves, and struggling to balance the competing demands of job performance, scholarship, and service with personal obligations. Candidates who are not recommended for promotion and tenure will remain colleagues—as a coworker, typically for one academic year, and as a professional colleague, perhaps for life. Helping a person to recover and begin again, despite any disappointment or anger he or she may exhibit, shows genuine kindness and care for the person as a human being. The rigor of a tenured position is not for everyone, and many academic libraries who do not follow a system of tenure may later view the unsuccessful tenure candidate as an attractive job prospect.

Summary

Systems of tenure or continuous appointment for librarians are commonplace in academe, but the processes and procedures in place to control such systems vary from situation to situation. These systems are in fact complex performance appraisals designed to make periodic and final personnel retention decisions. These systems are characterized by a long probationary period, an expectation that the employee will establish and document his or her own case for retention, the inclusion of external peer review, and layers of hierarchical review upward through the organization. Because the award of tenure or continuous appointment and advancement in rank are employment transactions, the institution has a responsibility to ensure that the system is fair, transparent, and consistent and that recommendations and decisions are based entirely on job-related factors.

REFERENCES

Academic Library Services. 2003. "Code of Operations." East Carolina University. www.ecu.edu/csacad/fsonline/customcf/unitcodes/academiclibraryservices .pdf.

American Association of University Professors. 1915. "Declaration of Principles on Academic Freedom and Academic Tenure." American Association of University Professors. www.aaup.org/AAUP/pubsres/policydocs/contents/1915.htm.

American Council on Education, American Association of University Professors, and United Educators Insurance Risk Retention Group. 2000. "Good Practice in Tenure Evaluation: Advice for Tenured Faculty, Department Chairs, and Academic Administrators." American Council on Education. www.acenet.edu/ bookstore/pdf/tenure-evaluation.pdf.

American University Library. 2011. "Guidelines for Tenure-Line Library Faculty Members for Reappointment and Promotion." American University. www .american.edu/provost/academicaffairs/upload/Library-Tenure-and -Promotion-Guidelienes-Final.pdf.

Association for College and Research Libraries. 2010. "A Guideline for the Appointment, Promotion and Tenure of Academic Librarians." American Library

Association. Approved in June. www.ala.org/acrl/standards/promotion tenure#tenure.

Boise State University Libraries. 2011. "Promotion and Tenure Guidelines." Boise State University. http://library.boisestate.edu/admin/tenure.pdf.

Coates Library. 2012. "Library Criteria for the Promotion and Tenure of Faculty Librarians: Library Faculty Research." Paper 16. Trinity University. http://digitalcommons.trinity.edu/lib_faculty/16.

Consortium Library. 2010. "Faculty Evaluation Criteria and Guidelines." University of Alaska Anchorage and Alaska Pacific University. June 16. www.uaa.alaska .edu/facultyservices/tenure/upload/Library-Promotion-Tenure-Guidelines-6 -15-10.pdf.

Indiana University Libraries. 2010. *IU Library Faculty Handbook*. Indiana University. www.iu.edu/~iulfc/IULibFacHandbook.pdf.

Louisiana State University Libraries. 2006. "Library Faculty Guidelines: Reappoint-ment, Promotion, and Tenure." Louisiana State University. Available on library intranet.

Nisonger, Thomas E., and Charles H. Davis. 2005. "The Perception of Library and Information Science Journals by LIS Education Deans and ARL Library Directors: A Replication of the Kohl-Davis Study." *College & Research Libraries* 66, no. 4: 341–377.

Office of the Vice Provost for Academic Affairs. 2009. "Frequently Asked Questions about Promotion and Tenure." Penn State University. Last updated May 28. www.psu.edu/vpaa/pdfs/p_and_t_faq.pdf.

Parker, Carol A. 2011. "Tenure Advice for Law Librarians and Their Directors." *Law Library Journal* 103, no. 2: 199–217.

Penn State University Libraries. 2010. "Human Resources Guideline UL-HRG07, Promotion and Tenure Criteria Guidelines." Last updated October 13. Penn State University. www.libraries.psu.edu/psul/policies/ulhrg07.html.

Stokes, Garnett S. 2012. "Making a Tenure Decision." In *Faculty Information*. Accessed February 2. http://provost.fsu.edu/faculty/tenure/decision.html.

Sun, Jeffrey C., and Steve Permuth. 2007. "Evaluations of Unionized College and University Faculty: A Review of the Laws." *Journal of Personnel Evaluation in Education* 19, no. 3/4: 115–134. doi:10.1007/s11092-007-9038-3.

University Library. 2008. "Statement of Promotion and Tenure to the Library Faculty at UIUC." University of Illinois at Urbana-Champaign. Last modified November 12. www.library.illinois.edu/committee/promo/pta.html.

University of Nebraska–Lincoln Libraries. 2007. "Promotion and Appointment Criteria." University of Nebraska–Lincoln. November 8. http://libraries.unl .edu/criteria.

concluding thoughts

Human resource management is the systematic recruitment, management, and direction of people for the purpose of achieving the mission and goals of an organization. HR management functions are practiced collaboratively at several levels within colleges and universities. Some functions of HR management are focused at the library level (supervision, performance evaluation, recruitment, discipline), some are impacted by processes at the academic level (recruitment, tenure, promotion), and some are administered at the campus level (compensation, benefits, labor relations, counseling and referral to employee assistance programs, compliance with state and federal employment laws). All of the functions require coordination and cooperation among the library, campus HR, the academic division, and the institution to operate the library successfully, to ensure consistency and fairness, and to protect the welfare of employees. The interplay of federal and state employment law and regulation, academic policy and tradition, ethics, and institutional culture and values all create the capacity for broad variation in local HR policies and practices. All the functions involve and affect each individual employee at one time or another.

Whatever an employee's involvement in the HR sphere—as an individual contributor, coworker, supervisor, search committee member or hiring manager, evaluator of faculty colleagues, or library manager or administrator, there are a few general principles useful for good practice.

Feedback is a gift. Whether it is from coworkers and colleagues, a supervisor or administrator, or from supervisees, authentic feedback is a gift offered by those who care about the library's success. Not all feedback is pleasant to receive or is delivered elegantly, but someone has taken the time to share an observation, and it usually contains a grain of truth. Like any gift, there is no obligation to accept it, but all feedback deserves consideration.

Hurry, but don't rush. Many times the need for HR answers, decisions, actions, or approval will be perceived as urgent by one party or another. People can be extremely distraught in times of personal challenge and press for an immediate response to their needs. They may present their preferred solution rather than explain all the details of the situation. Responding to pressure can lead to making regrettable judgments and taking unnecessary action and can further complicate an already confused situation. Take time to gather information, consult with others, and gain some emotional distance before taking action.

The person in need of immediate action might be understandably distraught, and this is a time the individual might benefit by stepping back and letting others work on his or her behalf. Before making rash statements, walking off the job, drawing out one's entire retirement account, or making any critical decisions, a conversation with someone in the library and the campus HR office might be beneficial. Knowledgeable library administrators and HR staff can help employees recognize that the most immediate action may not be in their best interests. Taking time to work with others to investigate all the possible options can lead to better problem resolution.

Consider the long-range impact of HR decisions. Exceptions can be made to some local rules or practices, but not to others. Local rules govern local practice; that is, they are operating rules created to address issues not determined by law or set by an authority, for example, a board of trustees or a university president. Consider whether the action will create a single-case exception to a rule, set a new precedent or lower an accepted standard, or undermine the basic purpose of the rule. If the action is not beneficial to either the library or an individual or group, then the rule might bear reconsideration. Assuming the action is lawful and the rule is not useful to anyone, then maybe it's time to abolish it. On the other hand, maybe there's a good reason for the rule, but it's not apparent until all the possible logical consequences of changing the rule are examined.

Employees asking for a rule change or an exception to policy might look at the situation from the library's perspective. Under what conditions would it be okay to except others from the rule? Is there any logical benefit of the rule for the library? Might there be a rule modification that would preserve the intent and effect of the rule but make it more reasonable to apply? There is value in the consistent application of rules but only if the rule makes sense and is effective in achieving its intended purpose.

Politely question the rules. The rules may have changed, or it may be possible to change them. Sometimes the rules are not even rules; the person or persons who made them may be long gone and no one even remembers why the rule was made in the first place, but the rule continues because no one questioned it. Because no one questioned it, managers and administrators might not be aware there is a problem.

Then question everything else. Asking questions is the best and fastest way to learn about institutional and library HR policies and practices. Even when presented in writing, a verbal explanation can assist in interpreting policy language, clarify the intended purpose, and simplify implementation. A full understanding of local HR policies and practices enables employees to act responsibly as individuals, as supervisors and managers, and as administrators to understand the rights and benefits of all employees. The best way to get specific, reliable answers to HR questions is to ask specific questions.

Don't take shortcuts. If there is a way to meet an HR objective quickly but it may not be entirely above board or it will work out only if it escapes review at a higher level, then it is not a good action to take. However inconvenient, ethical behavior requires following the necessary processes. If HR documentation of positions, new hires, or transactions for existing employees contains incorrect information or misrepresents the substance of the information, then it is likely to hurt the concerned parties somewhere down the line.

Cultivate a good relationship with the staff at campus HR. They are career professionals who are devoted full time to administering HR policies, to ensuring that the institution complies with applicable laws, and to working with troubled employees. They have experience with unusual circumstances and, in general, observe the highest standards of personal and professional behavior. They have encyclopedic knowledge of benefit programs and are the institutional authority for answering specific questions about health and other types of insurance, retirement systems, and paid and unpaid leave programs. Consulting HR experts prior to taking action, participating in the HR training offered, and acting in good faith will help establish campus HR as a valuable partner and perhaps even an advocate for the library.

No book can answer every HR question, especially when the range of human behavior and workplace experience is vast and some of the human variables are impenetrable or unknowable. We are, after all, only *human* resources.

about the author

Gail Munde is an assistant professor of library science at East Carolina University in Greenville, North Carolina. Prior to teaching, she worked in academic libraries for 25 years as a department chair and associate director/dean of libraries, holding positions at the University of Kansas, East Carolina University, and the University of Nevada, Las Vegas. She is a certified professional in human resources and received an MLS from Emporia State University and a PhD in library science from the University of North Texas.

index

Z

You may also be interested in

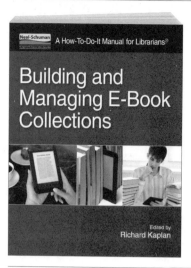

Building and Managing E-Book Collections: A How-To-Do-It Manual for Librarians

EDITED BY RICHARD KAPLAN

Beginning with a short history of e-books and a review of the e-book publishing industry and its effect on the library's selection and budget process, this how-to provides a thorough treatment of collection development issues

ISBN: 978-1-5557-0776-7
216 pages / 8.5" x 11"

WORKPLACE CULTURE IN ACADEMIC LIBRARIES: THE EARLY 21ST CENTURY
EDITED BY KELLY BLESSINGER AND PAUL HRYCAJ
ISBN: 978-1-84334-702-6

REFLECTING ON THE FUTURE OF ACADEMIC AND PUBLIC LIBRARIES
EDITED BY PETER HERNON AND JOSEPH R. MATTHEWS
ISBN: 978-0-8389-1187-7

GETTING STARTED WITH EVALUATION
PETER HERNON, ROBERT E. DUGAN, AND JOSEPH R. MATTHEWS
ISBN: 978-0-8389-1195-2

BUILD A GREAT TEAM: ONE YEAR TO SUCCESS
CATHERINE HAKALA-AUSPERK
ISBN: 978-0-8389-1170-9

BE A GREAT BOSS: ONE YEAR TO SUCCESS
CATHERINE HAKALA-AUSPERK
ISBN: 978-0-8389-1068-9

MENTORING AND MANAGING STUDENTS IN THE ACADEMIC LIBRARY
MICHELLE REALE
ISBN: 978-0-8389-1174-7

Order today at **alastore.ala.org** or **866-746-7252!**
ALA Store purchases fund advocacy, awareness, and accreditation programs for library professionals worldwide.